FOR EVERYONE
BIBLE STUDY GUIDES

•

JOHN

26 studies for individuals or groups

•

TOM WRIGHT

with
Kristie Berglund

Published in the United States of America in 2010 by
InterVarsity Press, P.O. Box 1400, Downers Grove, IL 60515-1426

Published in Great Britain in 2010

Society for Promoting Christian Knowledge
36 Causton Street
London SW1P 4ST
www.spckpublishing.co.uk

British Library Cataloguing-in-Publication Data
A catalogue record for this book is available from the British Library

ISBN 978–0–281–06225–6

First printed in Great Britain by Ashford Colour Press
Subsequently digitally printed in Great Britain

Produced on paper from sustainable forests

Contents

Getting the Most Out of John

The Gospel of John has always been a favorite. At one level it is the simplest of all the Gospels; at another level it is the most profound.

It gives the appearance of being written by someone who was a very close friend of Jesus, and who spent the rest of his life mulling over, more and more deeply, what Jesus had done and said and achieved, praying it through from every angle, and helping others to understand it. Countless people down the centuries have found that, through reading this Gospel, the figure of Jesus becomes real for them, full of light and warmth and promise. It is, in fact, one of the great books in the literature of the world; and part of its greatness is the way it reveals its secrets not just to those with high-flown learning, but to those who come to it with humility and hope.

The book opens with the unforgettable words: "In the beginning was the Word." At once we know that we are entering a place which is both familiar and strange. "In the beginning"—no Bible reader could see that phrase and not think at once of the start of Genesis, the first book of the Old Testament: "In the beginning God created the heavens and the earth." And it will do this through "the Word." In Genesis 1, the climax is the creation of humans, made in God's image. In John 1, the climax is the arrival of a human being, the Word become "flesh." Throughout this study we will see this and other themes from Genesis pop up from time to time. It is worth being alert for them. (For more on this book, also see my *John for Everyone: Part One* and *John for Everyone: Part Two,* published by SPCK and Westminster John Knox. This guide is based on those books and was prepared with the help of Kristie Berglund, for which I am grateful.)

Whatever else John is going to tell us, he wants us to see his book as the story of God and the world, not just the story of one character in one place and time. This book is about the Creator God acting in a new way within his much-loved creation. It is about the way in which the long story that began in Genesis has reached the climax the Creator always intended.

SUGGESTIONS FOR INDIVIDUAL STUDY

1. As you begin each study, pray that God will speak to you through his Word.

2. Read the introduction to the study and respond to the "Open" question that follows it. This is designed to help you get into the theme of the study.

3. Read and reread the Bible passage to be studied. Each study is designed to help you consider the meaning of the passage in its context. The commentary and questions in this guide are based on my own translation of each passage found in the companion volume to this guide in the For Everyone series on the New Testament (published by SPCK and Westminster John Knox).

4. Write your answers to the questions in a personal journal. Each study includes three types of questions: observation questions, which ask about the basic facts in the passage; interpretation questions, which delve into the meaning of the passage; and application questions, which help you discover the implications of the text for growing in Christ. Writing out your responses can bring clarity and deeper understanding of yourself and of God's Word.

5. Each session features selected comments from the For Everyone series. These notes provide further biblical and cultural background

and contextual information. They are designed not to answer the questions for you but to help you along as you study the Bible for yourself. For even more reflections on each passage, you may wish to have on hand a copy of the companion volume from the For Everyone series as you work through this study guide.

6. Use the guidelines in the "Pray" section to focus on God, thanking him for what you have learned and praying about the applications that have come to mind.

SUGGESTIONS FOR GROUP MEMBERS

1. Come to the study prepared. Follow the suggestions for individual study mentioned above. You will find that careful preparation will greatly enrich your time spent in group discussion.

2. Be willing to participate in the discussion. The leader of your group will not be lecturing. Instead, she or he will be asking the questions found in this guide and encouraging the members of the group to discuss what they have learned.

3. Stick to the topic being discussed. These studies focus on a particular passage of Scripture. Only rarely should you refer to other portions of the Bible or outside sources. This allows for everyone to participate on equal ground and for in-depth study.

4. Be sensitive to the other members of the group. Listen attentively when they describe what they have learned. You may be surprised by their insights! Each question assumes a variety of answers. Many questions do not have "right" answers, particularly questions that aim at meaning or application. Instead the questions push us to explore the passage more thoroughly.

   When possible, link what you say to the comments of others. Also, be affirming whenever you can. This will encourage some of the more hesitant members of the group to participate.

5. Be careful not to dominate the discussion. We are sometimes so eager to express our thoughts that we leave too little opportunity

for others to respond. By all means participate! But allow others to also.

6. Expect God to teach you through the passage being discussed and through the other members of the group. Pray that you will have an enjoyable and profitable time together, but also that as a result of the study you will find ways that you can take action individually and/ or as a group.

7. It will be helpful for groups to follow a few basic guidelines. These guidelines, which you may wish to adapt to your situation, should be read at the beginning of the first session.

    • Anything said in the group is considered confidential and will not be discussed outside the group unless specific permission is given to do so.

    • We will provide time for each person present to talk if he or she feels comfortable doing so.

    • We will talk about ourselves and our own situations, avoiding conversation about other people.

    • We will listen attentively to each other.

    • We will be very cautious about giving advice.

Additional suggestions for the group leader can be found at the back of the guide.

1

THE WORD MADE FLESH

John 1:1-18

Approaching John's Gospel is a bit like arriving at a grand, imposing house. Many Bible readers know that this Gospel is not quite like the others. They may have heard, or begun to discover, that it's got hidden depths of meaning. According to one well-known saying, this book is like a pool that's safe for a child to paddle in but deep enough for an elephant to swim in. But, though it's imposing in its structure and ideas, it's not meant to scare you off. It makes you welcome. Indeed, millions have found that, as they come closer to this book, the Friend above all friends is coming out to meet them.

Like many a grand house, the book has a driveway, bringing you off the main road, telling you something about the place you're getting to before you get there. These opening verses are, in fact, such a complete introduction to the book that by the time you get to the story you know a good deal about what's coming, and what it means.

OPEN

Have you ever felt intimidated walking up to a large or important house or building? Why is this sometimes so daunting?

STUDY

1. *Read John 1:1-18.* As noted in the introduction, the first words of John's Gospel—"In the beginning"—echo the opining of the start of Genesis, the first book in the Old Testament: "In the beginning, God created the heavens and the earth." Why does John begin his story of Jesus with this reference to the story of creation?

2. When I speak a word, it is, in a sense, part of me. When people hear it they assume that I intended it: "But you said . . ." People will comment if our deeds don't match up to our words. What do our words reveal about our hearts and our character?

3. In the Old Testament, God regularly acts by means of his "word." What he says, happens—in Genesis itself, and regularly thereafter. "By the word of the LORD," says the psalm, "the heavens were made" (33:6 RSV). God's word is the one thing that will last, even though people and plants wither and die (Isaiah 40:6-8). God's word will go out of his mouth and bring life, healing and hope to Israel and the whole creation (Isaiah 55:10-11).

   How does this Old Testament background help us understand what John is trying to tell us about the "Word [who] became flesh" (v. 14)?

4. Verses 1-2 and 18 begin and end the passage by stressing that the Word was and is God, and is intimately close to God. Why does John emphasize this so strongly?

5. This is the theme of John's gospel: If you want to know who the true God is, look long and hard at Jesus. How does our understanding of God get off track when we try to think about who he is apart from Jesus?

6. The Word challenged the darkness before creation and now challenges the darkness that is found, tragically, within creation itself. The Word is bringing into being the new creation, in which God says once more, "Let there be light!" How did the darkness respond to the coming of this new light (vv. 5, 9-10)?

7. In what ways does the darkness either fail to understand or actively resist the light of Christ in our own lives and in the world around us?

8. Perhaps the most exciting thing about this opening passage is that we're in it too: "To anyone who did accept him" (v. 12)—that means anyone at all, then and now. You don't have to be born into a particular family or part of the world. God wants people from everywhere to be born in a new way, born into the family he began through Jesus and which has since spread through the world. Anyone can become

a "child of God" in this sense, a sense which goes beyond the fact that all humans are special in God's sight. Something can happen to people in this life which causes them to become new people, people who (as v. 12 says) "believe in his name."

How does believing in the name of Jesus transform someone's life so that he or she becomes a new person?

9. Have you experienced this or seen it happen in the lives of others?

10. Somehow the great drama of God and the world, of Jesus and Israel, of the Word who reveals the glory of the unseen God—this great drama is a play in search of actors, and there are great parts for everyone, you and me included. Why would God choose to include human beings in his great drama of salvation?

11. What part do you play in this drama?

PRAY

Give thanks to God for once again speaking light into darkness, for sending Jesus to live among us and show us very clearly who God is. Ask God to lead you deeper into his fullness and grace and to help you find your place in his great drama.

2

THE BAPTIST
AND THE DISCIPLES

John 1:19-51

I want to make it quite clear that I'm not a candidate."

You hear that said over and over as politicians jostle for position before a major election. No, they aren't going to stand. No, they have no intention of running for office. No, they are going to sit this one out. And then—surprise, surprise—suddenly they make a speech saying that friends have advised them, that pressure has been put on them, that for the good of the country they now intend . . . to run after all. And we have become quite cynical about it all.

But here we have a story about a man pushing himself forward in the public eye, gaining a large following and then refusing to claim any of the offices they were eager to ascribe to him.

OPEN

Do your political or religious leaders ever behave in ways that cause you to become disheartened or cynical? What are some specific examples of this?

STUDY

1. *Read John 1:19-34.* A group of priests and Levites—temple function-
    aries—came to check John out, sent by the Pharisees who were one
    of the leading pressure groups of the time. What are John the Bap-
    tist's responses when the religious leaders ask him who he is?

For centuries the Jews had read in the Bible that the great prophet,
Elijah, would return before the great and terrible "day of the LORD"
(Malachi 4:5). Elijah, it seemed, hadn't died in an ordinary way,
but had been taken up into heaven directly (2 Kings 2). Now, many
believed, he would return to herald God's new day. Indeed many
Christians, and most likely Jesus as well, believed that John was in
fact Elijah, even if he didn't think so—a puzzle to which the New
Testament offers no solution (see, e.g., Mark 9:13). But, anyway, John
clearly didn't want anyone thinking he was Elijah.

Elijah wasn't the only great prophet. Most in Jesus' day would
have ranked him second to Moses himself. In Deuteronomy 18:15-18
God promises that he will raise up a prophet like Moses to lead
the people. This figure, a yet-to-come "prophet like Moses," was ex-
pected in Jesus' day (see John 6:14), though most people probably
didn't distinguish sharply between the different "figures" they had
heard or read about. Enough to know that *someone* would come, and
preferably soon, to sort out the mess they were in.

2. What do we learn about the character of John the Baptist from his
    refusal to accept any of these prestigious titles?

3. One of the many points to ponder about the strange character of John
    the Baptist is the way in which all Christian preachers are called to
    the same attitude that John had. We don't preach ourselves, as Paul

said, but we preach Jesus Christ as Lord, and ourselves as your servants for his sake (2 Corinthians 4:5). Or, as John put it, "I'm only a
voice."

How might we follow the example of John the Baptist in our own
lives?

4. Israel's Scriptures hadn't spoken of a prophet who would come and
    plunge people into water. What was John's baptism designed to pre-
    pare the people of Israel for (vv. 26, 31)?

5. In what ways are we—the readers of John's Gospel today—in need
    of preparation to encounter the One whom John speaks of?

6. The death of Jesus takes place, in this Gospel, on the afternoon
    when the Passover lambs were being killed in the temple. Jesus is
    the true Passover lamb. John wants us to understand the events con-
    cerning Jesus as a new, and better, exodus story. Just as God brought
    the children of Israel out of Egypt, so God was now bringing a new
    people out of an even older and darker slavery.

    What slavery does this new exodus set us free from?

7. *Read John 1:35-51.* Why do John the Baptist's disciples begin to follow Jesus (vv. 36-37)?

8. Why does Jesus give Simon a new name, and what does his new name signify (v. 42)?

9. This passage introduces us to a shadowy character who is going to flit across the pages of this Gospel several times. There were two disciples of John the Baptist who heard him pointing to Jesus as God's lamb. Only one is named: Andrew (v. 40). Who might the other disciple be, and why do you think he remains unnamed?

10. Nathanael, who comes from Cana (John tell us this in 21:2), can't believe that anything good would come out of the rival village, Nazareth, a short distance up the hill (v. 46).

    What kinds of prejudices prevent people from seeking Jesus today?

11. Verse 51 seems to be a tightly packed and evocative way of saying: "Don't think that all you'll see is one or two remarkable acts of insight, such as you witnessed when I showed you that I knew about you before you even appeared. What you'll see from now on is the reality toward which Jacob's ladder (Genesis 28:10-22), and even the

temple itself, was pointing like a signpost. If you follow me, you'll be watching what it looks like when heaven and earth are open to each other."

What does it mean that Jesus has made heaven and earth open to each other?

12. Are there any ordinary people—like Andrew, Simon Peter, Nathanael or the unnamed disciple—in your life that you might consider inviting to "come and see" Jesus so that they too might experience what it's like for heaven and earth to be opened to each other right before their eyes? If so, what kind of "come and see" invitation might you make?

PRAY

Give thanks to God for giving Jesus to be the great Passover lamb who takes away the sin of the whole world and for sending his Spirit to live in us. Ask him to grant you a deep humility in which you live only to point away from yourself and toward Christ—just like John the Baptist did. Ask God also to make you bold to extend the invitation to others to encounter Jesus for themselves.

3

A WEDDING
AND A COMMOTION

John 2

One of the first events I ever organized was a treasure hunt. It was during the school holidays, when I was about ten or eleven. I invited all my friends from neighboring houses and streets to come and join in.

With my mother's careful help, I planned each of the clues in cryptic rhyming couplets, and worked out the different things people would find as they followed them. I remember feeling nervous as fifteen or twenty children poured out of the house eager to follow up the clues they had been given. Would they understand them all right? Would they get bored and give up? Would some be much better at it than others? I needn't have worried. The event was a success and everyone had fun.

John's Gospel is a kind of treasure hunt, with careful, sometimes cryptic clues laid for us to follow. Now that he's set the scene with stories about John the Baptist and Jesus' early followers, he gives us the first clue, telling us that it's the first one so we know where we are.

OPEN

Have you ever been involved in a treasure hunt? What did you find exciting about it? What did you find difficult or frustrating?

STUDY

1. *Read John 2:1-12.* Running out of wine was not just inconvenient, but a social disaster and disgrace. The family would have to live with the shame of it for a long time to come; bride and groom might regard it as bad luck on their married life. What is Jesus' first response when his mother asks him to do something about this crisis (v. 4)?

2. What might have motivated Jesus to act despite the fact that he believed his "time" hadn't come yet?

3. This is only one of two occasions we meet Jesus' mother in John's Gospel, the other being at the foot of the cross (John 19). How do these two events act as a set of bookends to John's Gospel?

4. The Old Testament commonly compares God to a bridegroom and Israel to his bride. John's readers would thus recognize a wedding as a foretaste of the great heavenly wedding feast in store for God's people (Revelation 21:2). The water jars, used for Jewish purification rites, are a sign that God is doing a new thing from within the old Jewish system, bringing purification to Israel and the world in a whole new way.

   How does the image of a wedding help us understand what's in store for God's people?

5. The word John uses for "clue" is *sign* (v. 11). He is setting up a series of signposts to take us through his story. They are moments when, to people who watch with at least a little faith, the angels are going up and coming down at the place where Jesus is. They are moments when heaven is opened, when the transforming power of God's love bursts in to the present world.

   How is this sign at the wedding an example of the transforming power of God's love?

6. What do you think John is hinting at when he says that this first sign took place "on the third day" (v. 1)?

7. The transformation from water to wine is of course meant by John to signify the effect that Jesus can have on people's lives. Where do we see Jesus' transforming power at work in our world today?

8. *Read John 2:13-25.* The temple was the beating heart of Judaism. It was the center of worship and music, of politics and society, of national celebration and mourning. It was the place where Israel's God, YHWH, had promised to live in the midst of his people. What do Jesus' words and actions tell us about what the temple had become (vv. 15-16)?

9. How might you have responded if you had been a Jew worshiping in the temple on that day?

There is no doubt what John thinks it all means. It is Passover time. He has already told us that Jesus is God's Passover lamb (1:29), and now he goes to Jerusalem at the time when liberation, freedom, rescue from slavery in Egypt (the exodus) was being celebrated. Somehow, John wants us to understand, what Jesus did in the temple is a hint at the new meaning he is giving to Passover.

10. When the Judeans ask Jesus what he thinks he's up to and request some kind of sign to show them what it all means, how does he respond?

11. In what ways is Jesus a far superior temple to the one he condemned in Jerusalem?

12. As so often, John ends with a hint as to how people should respond. If you see the signs that Jesus is doing, then trust him. Believe in him. Jesus, after all, is the one who knows us through and through.

At this point in your encounters with Jesus through John's Gospel, what is your response to him and his signs?

PRAY

Pray through these stories with your own failures and disappointments in mind, remembering that the transformation of water to wine came only when someone took Mary's words seriously: "Do whatever he tells you." Take time to consider before God that though Jesus condemned something important that had become corrupt, he didn't leave the people empty-handed. Instead, he gave them something much greater —himself.

JESUS AND NICODEMUS

John 3

I have lost my birth certificate.

It's the sort of thing that happens when you move to a new house, which we did not long ago. I know where it was in the old house. It may have been accidentally thrown away; but I suspect it was put into a very, very safe place, and the place was so safe that I still haven't found it.

Fortunately, I don't need it at the moment. I have a passport and other documents. Sooner or later, if it doesn't show up, I shall have to get a replacement, which means going back to the town where I was born and paying to have a new copy made from the register there.

But, of course, the one thing that a birth certificate isn't needed for is to prove that a birth took place. Here I am, a human being; obviously I must have been born. The fact that at the moment I can't officially prove when and where is a minor detail.

When Christians discuss the "new birth," the "second birth" or the "birth from above," they often forget this.

OPEN

Stories of births are often characterized by a combination of anxiety, humor, joy and pain. What details do you know about your own birth?

STUDY

1. *Read John 3:1-21.* The Judaism that Nicodemus and Jesus both knew had a good deal to do with being born into the right family. What mattered was being a child of Abraham. Why did Nicodemus find Jesus' words so difficult to believe?

2. How do cultural values sometimes keep us from understanding and embracing Jesus' message?

The new birth Jesus is talking about is the same thing that has been spoken of in 1:33. "Water and spirit" here must mean the double baptism: baptism in water, which brings people into the visible community of Jesus' followers (3:22; 4:1-2), *and* baptism in the Spirit, which gives the new life of the Spirit welling up like a spring of water inside, are both required for entrance into God's kingdom.

As with 1:12-13, the point of this is that God's kingdom is now thrown open to anyone and everyone. The Spirit is on the move, like a fresh spring breeze, and no human family, tribe, organization or system can keep up with it. Opening the window and letting the breeze in can be very inconvenient, especially for the Nicodemuses of this world who suppose they have got things tidied up, labeled and sorted into neat piles.

3. In verses 10-13, we have the first of many passages in which Jesus speaks about a new knowledge—indeed a new sort of knowing. What do we learn about this new sort of knowing?

4. How does John's Gospel suggest we will gain this new knowledge, and what difference will it make in our lives?

5. Verse 14 looks back to the incident described in Numbers 21:5-8. What is Jesus ("the son of man") compared to in that story?

6. How is the crucifixion of Jesus like putting the snake on a pole?

7. How is this peculiar cure a demonstration of the greatness of God's love for the world (v. 16)?

What John is saying, and will continue to say right up to his account of the crucifixion, is that the evil which was and is in the world, deep-rooted within us all, was somehow allowed to take out its full force on Jesus. When we look at him hanging on the cross, what we are looking at is the result of the evil in which we are all stuck. And we are seeing what God has done about it.

8. What is at the very heart of John's amazing new picture of God?

9.   Precisely because evil lurks deep within each of us, for healing to
     take place we must be involved in the process. That doesn't mean
     that we just have to try a lot harder to be good. What is required of
     us (vv. 18, 21)?

10. *Read John 3:22-36.* What does John say to settle down his disciples
     about the success of Jesus?

11. Sometimes different churches or Christian groups are jealous of
     each other's success. What does this passage have to teach us?

12. Instead of family rivalries, where do verses 31-36 say our focus
     should be?

PRAY

Thank God for loving the world so much that he lifted up the Son on
the cross, giving us the chance to look on him in faith and be healed of
all the evil that lurks deep within us. Pray that we and all those around
us may feel the wind of his Spirit and experience the brand new life that
he brings.

NOTE ON JOHN 3:22-36

The picture of the bridegroom with his bride is not just a convenient illustration, showing that John's followers are jealous of Jesus and that John is refusing to see things in those terms. In the Old Testament and some Jewish traditions, the coming Messiah was seen as the bridegroom par excellence, the one who would come and make Israel his bride. Behind this again, of course, is the equally important tradition that YHWH, Israel's God, would betroth Israel to himself as his bride. Whether or not the Baptist thought of this at the time—his mind seems to be focused on the fact that Jesus is Israel's Messiah, the coming king, and that he himself is not—the writer certainly intends us to think so.

John the evangelist also intends for us to see, not for the last time in the Gospel, the way in which different characters in the story of Jesus have to learn, as C. S. Lewis once put it, to play great parts without pride and small parts without shame. At the very end of the Gospel (21:20-23), Peter is reminded that what counts is not comparing yourself with other people and seeing whether your status is higher or lower than theirs, but simply following Jesus. Here, already, John the Baptist adds to the evidence he's given about Jesus' messiahship by insisting that if Jesus is prospering, and people are going to him, that means that he, who had pointed to him, should celebrate rather than be miserable or jealous.

THE WOMAN OF SAMARIA

John 4:1-42

A friend of mine described the reaction when he went home, as a young teenager, and announced to his mother that he'd become a Christian. Alarmed, she thought he'd joined some kind of cult. "They've brainwashed you!" she said.

He was ready with the right answer. "If you'd seen what was in my brain," he replied, "you'd realize it needed washing!"

Of course, he hadn't been brainwashed. In fact, again and again—and this was certainly the case for my friend—when people bring their lives into the light of Jesus the Messiah, things begin to come clear.

Often when this begins, the reaction is like that of the Samaritan woman we meet in John 4. Intrigued by Jesus' offer of "living water," she asks to have some—not realizing that if you want the running, pure water, bubbling up inside you that Jesus offers, you will have to get rid of the stale, moldy water you've been living off of all this time.

OPEN

Have your family or friends ever been shocked when you changed your mind about something or took an unexpected new direction in life? Describe the situation.

STUDY

1. *Read John 4:1-42.* The picture we see at the beginning of this passage (vv. 1-15) has several things "wrong" with it. They may not look odd to us, but we only understand the passage when we see how it would have looked to anyone at the time it was written.

   What in this story would have seemed strange, unconventional or just plain wrong to people living in Jesus' time and culture (v. 9)?

2. Why does Jesus invite such an unconventional interaction with the Samaritan woman?

3. How might following Jesus require us to behave in ways our culture finds strange or disturbing?

4. What misunderstandings arise between Jesus and the woman in verses 1-15?

   Again and again in this Gospel Jesus talks to people who misunderstand what he says. He is talking at the heavenly level and they are listening at the earthly level. But because the one God created both heaven and earth, and because the point of Jesus' work is precisely to bring the life of heaven to earth, the misunderstandings are, in that sense, "natural."

5. What does Jesus say this living water will do inside the woman?

6. Why does the woman change the subject once Jesus demonstrates how much he knows about her personal life (vv. 19-20)?

7. How does Jesus respond to her excuses?

8. What excuses or differences of opinion do people offer today for not seeking God?

God's claim on every human life—and God's offer of a new kind of human life for all who give up the stagnant water and come to him for the living variety—is absolute, and can't be avoided by questions about which church people think they should go to, any more than Jesus' claim on this woman's moral conscience could be avoided by the debate, already hundreds of years old, as to whether Mount Zion in Jerusalem or Mount Gerizim in Samaria was the true holy mountain.

In fact, part of the point of Jesus' mission, to bring the life of heaven to birth on earth, was that from now on holy mountains wouldn't matter that much. Holy buildings and holy mountains are at best only signposts to the real thing. If they become substitutes for it, you're in trouble. That way lies idolatry, the worship of something that isn't God as if it were.

9. Why does Jesus bring up the point that "God is spirit" and that those who worship him must do so "in spirit and in truth" (v. 24)?

10. What is Jesus' response when the disciples urge him to eat something (vv. 32, 34-38)?

11. What in particular might have prompted this unexpected response?

12. When you look on the harvest waiting to be gathered, how do you feel? Excited? Motivated? Overwhelmed? Scared? Explain.

13. The way the passage ends is worth pondering deeply. Here is a woman who, a matter of an hour or so before, had been completely trapped in a life of immorality, as a social outcast. Now she had become the first evangelist to the Samaritan people. Before any of Jesus' own followers could do it, she has told them that he is the Messiah. And then, as they have come to see Jesus for themselves, they have become convinced.

    How have encounters with Jesus transformed you in unexpected ways?

PRAY

Take a moment to reflect on Jesus' offer of living water that he extends to us just as he did to the Samaritan woman. Ask the Lord that you also may drink of this water and discover its healing, life-giving, transforming power.

NOTE ON JOHN 4:10

"Living water" is the regular phrase people used in Jesus' world for what we call running water—water in a stream or river, rather than a pool or well, water that's more likely to be fresh and clean than water that's been standing around getting stagnant. But here the double meaning kicks into operation; because of course Jesus isn't referring to physical water, whether still or moving. He is referring to the new life that he is offering to anyone: as this conversation shows, anyone at all, no matter what their gender, their geography, their racial or moral background.

TWO HEALINGS

John 4:43—5:9

Imagine a town planner designing a new set of road signs to get people round the streets in the quickest and easiest fashion. The town is old, famous and beautiful, and nothing but very fine and well-designed signs will do for such a setting. But when the signs are put up, you discover that everyone is stopping and getting out of their cars to stand and admire the signs. Instead of the traffic flowing smoothly by, it's getting clogged up worse than before.

Let's put it another way, this time in terms of the big picture John is showing us. The Word has become flesh. But suppose people admire the flesh so much that they forget about the Word. That, it seems, is the danger Jesus is now facing—and will continue to face through the next seven chapters, as the sequence of "signs" unfolds before our eyes.

OPEN

Have you ever totally missed the point of something? How did you feel when you realized this?

STUDY

1. *Read John 4:43—5:9.* Verses 44-45 in chapter 4 may seem a bit puzzling: it looks as though John is first saying that prophets aren't
   honored in their own country. But then the Galileans, Jesus' own
   countrymen and countrywomen, welcome him, remembering the
   things he had done in Jerusalem.

   What does Jesus' response to the people in verse 48 tell us about how
   he perceived their welcome?

2. Why did Jesus perform signs if he didn't want people to follow him
   for the wrong reasons?

3. How are we today sometimes guilty of following Jesus for the wrong
   reasons?

4. How is the response of the official in verses 50 and 53 an example of
   what Jesus was desiring?

5. Why does John emphasize the distinction between believing because we've seen something and believing on the strength of Jesus'
   words?

6. How might we follow the example of the official?

7. The pool of Bethesda was a well-known place of healing. It was in Jerusalem itself, just to the north of the temple mount area. But it wasn't just a Jewish healing place. The evidence suggests that pagans too regarded it as a sacred site. At one stage it was dedicated to the healing god Asclepius.

   The way it worked seems to have been like this: The waters in the pool would bubble up periodically; when that happened, the first person to get in would be healed. Some people reckoned that the bubbling water was caused by an angel. But the shrine didn't seem particularly successful. Clearly the man Jesus found lying there had made a way of life out of his long wait for healing.

   How long had the man Jesus encounters been lying sick beside the pool (v. 5)?

8. Why does Jesus ask him if he wants to be made well?

9. How do sins, problems or sicknesses become so much part of our identity that we have trouble letting them go?

As with many of the gospel stories, particularly in John, what Jesus does fulfills the hopes and longings of the Jewish world. Here, however, Jesus seems to be fulfilling the hopes and half-formed beliefs of the pagan world as well. The pagan shrine points dimly to the healing that Jesus was bringing.

Paganism looks at the world of creation and tries to harness forces within it for its own ends. The healing that Jesus offers is the reality that the created world was waiting for, the beginning of the new creation. The salvation that the Son of God brings when he comes into the world is the new day that, had they known it, Israel and the world had been longing for.

10. How does Jesus' command to "get up" give us a hint at what his new creation will look like?

11. What in particular do you look forward to being healed and freed from in the new creation that Jesus brings?

PRAY

Ponder the signs in these stories and allow them to point you to Christ. Ask God to help you to hear the words Jesus speaks to you and to simply believe him—to take him at his word as the official did when his son was healed. Pray that Jesus would set you free from enduring sins and sicknesses and bid you "get up" to walk with him in newness of life.

7

Jesus and the Father

John 5:9-47

I woke up to hear a voice speaking a language I didn't understand. Where was I? What was going on? A dim light from the other side of the room reminded me. I was at the conference. I was sharing a room with a colleague from the university, a distinguished Indian scholar, who taught Hinduism.

It was four o'clock in the morning where we were, and he was on the telephone with his wife. It was already seven o'clock in Montreal, and she would be getting up with the children. He wanted her to know we were safe. He came off the phone.

I chided him. "Come on! It's four in the morning! It's time for rest!"

"No," he said, "it's time to wake up—at least it is at home! My wife has to get off to work and I had to speak to her."

In John 5 Jesus and his Judean opponents are working in two different time zones. Not geographical time zones, of course. Rather, they were in what you might call different *theological* time zones.

OPEN

Have you ever experienced time-zone confusion—perhaps while you were traveling somewhere or while a friend or loved one you wanted to contact was far away?

STUDY

1. *Read John 5:9-47.* As we discover in the Old Testament, one of the original purposes of sabbath was to highlight the seventh day as the time when the Creator God rested from his work in making the world. Week by week, the law-observant Jews kept a strict day without work—defining quite carefully what "work" might include so there would be no doubt.

   What is Jesus' response when the Judeans confront him about breaking the sabbath (vv. 16-17)?

2. What does Jesus' response mean and why does it make his opponents so angry (v. 18)?

3. What would it look like for us to be the followers of Jesus who are always prepared to say, "Jesus is at work, and so am I"?

4. Verses 19-23 seem to be almost a parable, a story about how sons can be apprenticed to their fathers; though of course the particular father and son here are God and Jesus.

   What is the most astonishing thing that the Son sees the Father doing (v. 21)?

5. It was already a popular belief in Jesus' day that God would raise the dead. There would come a day, they believed, when God would make everything right. God the Creator would bring people back into bodily life, to face the consequences of their evil deeds, or share the rewards of their righteous ones. What Jesus is now saying is that with his coming and public ministry *this work of raising the dead has already begun.*

    What examples in John's Gospel (or the other Gospels) can you think of that demonstrate Jesus' work of giving life, hints that point to raising the dead way before any of the Jews of his day expected this to happen?

6. In what way do the followers of Christ experience the miracle of resurrection even prior to their physical death and resurrection?

7. Bringing new creation to birth can only be done if the evil that has corrupted the old creation is named, shamed and dealt with. That's what judgment is all about.

    How does understanding this help us to live in a world where tyranny and injustice are still rampant?

8. Frequently in John's Gospel we have the sense that we are specta-
    tors in a court of law. John keeps on talking about "evidence" or,
    as it's sometimes translated, "testimony" or "witness." At this stage
    it looks as though Jesus is on trial, though it's not clear what the
    charge is.

    What evidence does Jesus suggest is even more important than that
    which John the Baptist gave on his behalf (vv. 36-37)?

9. Why is it so difficult for Jesus' opponents to accept this evidence?

10. The worrying thing is that it wasn't just a problem for people to
    accept this evidence in Jesus' day. John sees this as a problem the
    whole world faces. Once the story of Jesus has been told, the jury is
    out—on the hearers, not on Jesus himself.

    What evidence about Jesus do people find persuasive today, and
    what evidence is unconvincing to them?

11. Why does Jesus tell his opponents that Moses himself condemns
    them (vv. 45-46)?

12. Jesus' charge to his contemporaries is that they have been looking at the right book but reading it the wrong way. How might this serve as a warning for us today in our own practice of reading, studying, sharing, teaching or preaching the Bible?

PRAY

Reflect on your own response to the evidence you have encountered about Jesus so far in John's Gospel. Give thanks to God for the way he brings new, resurrection life even into the midst of this yet broken world, and ask him for a heart that is willing to believe in the evidence about his Son and trust in him alone.

NOTE ON JOHN 5:17

The sabbath originated in Genesis 2:1-7, a day of rest after the six days in which God completed the work of creation. Jesus believed that Israel's God was now in the process of launching the *new creation*. And somehow this new creation was superseding the old one. Its time scale was taking precedence. God was healing the sorry, sick world, and though there might come a time for rest (when Jesus' own work was finished, maybe: see 19:28-30), at the moment it was time for the work of the new creation to go forward. Especially, from John's point of view, if the "signs" correspond in some way to the "days" of the new creation.

8

TWO SIGNS

John 6:1-25

When you read detective stories, you quickly learn that what may look like an irrelevant little detail may actually be the clue to discovering who the murderer really is. A good writer will put in all kinds of detail, designed to lead the eye and the mind in several directions; nothing is there by accident. But somewhere in the middle is the sign that, if only you'd been thinking hard about it at the time, will tell you the secret.

Nothing in John's Gospel is there by accident. John 6 is the second time John has told us of something happening at Passover time; the previous time was when Jesus was in Jerusalem casting out the traders in the temple (2:13). There will be a third time, when Jesus arrives in Jerusalem for the last time, and then it is so important for John's understanding of what is about to happen that he mentions it three times (11:55; 12:1; 13:1). This is no detective story; John is not trying to keep us guessing. He wants us to understand, as we go along, where it is all going.

OPEN

Think of a favorite detective story or mystery. What is it about the story that you like so much?

STUDY

1. *Read John 6:1-25.* John 5 ends with Jesus saying Moses was writing about him. In these opening passages of John 6, we will see two examples of that.

   What does Jesus suggest that he and his disciples need to do for the great crowd that has gathered around them (v. 5)?

2. Why might this have sounded a bit crazy to his disciples?

3. Philip doesn't know what to do. Andrew doesn't either, but he brings the boy with his bread and fish to Jesus' attention. The point is obvious, but we perhaps need to be reminded of it: so often we ourselves have no idea what to do, but the starting point is always to bring what is there to the attention of Jesus. You can never tell what he's going to do with it, though part of the Christian faith is the expectation that he will do something we hadn't thought of—something new and creative.

   How might Andrew have felt when he brought the boy and his meager lunch to the attention of Jesus?

4. Are there things in your life—things that perhaps you consider to be of little value—that you might bring to Jesus, expecting that he could do something new and creative and wonderful with them?

5. God fed the children of Israel, during their wilderness wanderings, with "bread from heaven." The story is told in Exodus 16, where the "manna" is provided by God through Moses because the people are grumbling and complaining.

   What similarities and differences are there between this story from Exodus and John's story of Jesus feeding the five thousand?

6. The five thousand being fed by Jesus knew about Moses and quickly make the jump from Jesus being a "prophet" to "Messiah"; in other words, to "king." How does the reaction of the crowds (v. 15) show that they don't really understand what these terms mean for Jesus?

7. In what ways are we guilty of this today—that is, how do we also sometimes try to "seize" Jesus and make him fit into our boxes instead of letting him have his say?

The children of Israel began their journey to freedom by coming through the Red Sea, with the waters parting before them but closing again on their pursuers. It was, of course, Moses who led the way through the Red Sea, and the crowds have just declared that Jesus is the prophet who is to come into the world—the prophet, that is, like Moses (v. 14; see Deuteronomy 18:15).

The crowds have misunderstood what such a prophet might have come to do—they were looking for another act of political liberation, but Jesus was offering something far greater. Jesus nevertheless does something which the disciples, in subsequent reflection, are bound to see in terms of the Exodus story, the Passover story.

8. How do the disciples react when they first see Jesus walking toward them in the midst of the storm (v. 19)?

9. What happens as soon as Jesus gets into the boat (v. 21)?

10. How is this event similar to Exodus 14 (especially vv. 10-18) when Moses leads Israel out of Egypt through the Red Sea?

11. There are many times when suddenly it seems the wind gets up and the sea becomes rough. As we struggle to make our way through, sometimes we are aware of a presence with us, which may initially be more disturbing than comforting. But if we listen, through the

roar of the waves and the wind, we may hear the voice that says, "It's me—don't be afraid!"

How might we prepare now to take Jesus on board the next time the winds pick up and the sea becomes rough for us?

PRAY

Reflect on these two stories with your own inadequacies and fears in mind. Bring what little you have to offer before the Lord in prayer, just as Andrew and the boy offered what little they had to him, and then wait in expectation for him to do marvelous things. Give thanks to him for the way he still comes to us in the midst of our rough seas. Ask that he would help you to receive his invitation to trust in him and not be afraid.

9

EATING AND DRINKING THE SON OF MAN

John 6:26-71

The historian was in a hurry to finish his Ph.D. There was one chapter to go, which concerned the painting that had been so important during his period, and the influence the artists had on the wider thought and culture of the time.

He went hastily from gallery to gallery. In every room he walked around beside the walls, scribbling in his notebook, taking down all the details from the printed notices underneath the paintings. He wrote down the artists' names, their dates, where they lived, the names of their key paintings, who their friends were, what influence others had on them, and they on others. As soon as he was finished he went onto the next gallery.

He finished his Ph.D. But at no time, in all the art galleries, had he ever stood back and looked at the paintings themselves, and allowed them to speak in their own language.

Jesus is clearly anxious that the people whom he had fed with the loaves and fishes are going to end up like that unfortunate historian.

OPEN

Have you ever visited an art gallery? What did you enjoy most about the experience?

STUDY

1. *Read John 6:26-46.* At first sight Jesus' warning in verses 26-27 seems almost churlish. He has done something remarkable; the crowds are excited and come to him wanting more; and he all but rebukes them for having the wrong motivation.

   What is wrong with the crowd's motivation for following Jesus?

2. What specifically does Jesus say that God wants from the people (v. 29)?

   It seems odd that they ask for a further sign, when Jesus has just given them one. Perhaps they were hoping for some action against the Roman occupiers, something more obviously military and political. Perhaps they wanted Jesus to march on Jerusalem and make the walls fall down, as Joshua had done with Jericho at the conclusion of the exodus.

3. In verse 35 Jesus gives the first of several famous "I am" sayings in the gospel. ("I am" is one of the central meanings of YHWH, or Yah-

weh, the secret and holy name of God uttered in Exodus 3:14.) This one is so important that it is repeated twice, in verses 48 and 51. What does Jesus mean by it?

4. One of the hard lessons the children of Israel had to learn in the wilderness was that their God, YHWH, was not at their beck and call. He wasn't obliged to them. It was simply that in his loving choice he had decided to make them his own people, so that they would be the nation through whom his purposes and love would be made known to the world.

   How does Jesus make this same point to the crowds in this passage (vv. 37-40)?

"Eternal life" (v. 40) is the quality of life, sharing the inner life of Jesus, that is on offer at once to anyone who believes. "Eternal" tells you what sort of life it is, as well as the fact that it goes on after death: it is the life of the age to come, the new life which God has always planned to give the world. But the form that this eternal life will take in the end is not that of the disembodied spirit that so many today assume is what Christians think about life after death. The eternal life that begins in the present when someone believes, and continues into the future beyond death, will eventually take the form of the resurrection life already spoken of in 5:25-29.

5. How do the Judeans respond to Jesus' words to them (v. 41)?

6. In what ways have you grumbled against God, just like the Israelites in the wilderness and the Judeans in this story?

7. When Jesus quotes "they shall all be taught by God" (v. 45) from Isaiah 54:13, he is calling to mind one of the Old Testament's greatest prophecies of the renewal that will come about through the outpouring of God's love, bringing his people back from exile. Part of the point of the Isaiah passage is the complete helplessness of Israel at the time. That's why God must take the initiative.

    In what way were the Judeans in this passage just as helpless and in need of God's initiative as the people of Israel in exile in Isaiah's time?

8. *Read John 6:47-71.* What does Jesus say that causes a great squabble among the Judeans (v. 52) and why are they so upset?

9. How do you respond to Jesus' words about eating his flesh and drinking his blood?

10. John understands Jesus' language here to refer to the Eucharist, the Lord's Supper, the sacrament in which Jesus' body and blood are, in a mysterious way, offered to believers to be eaten and drunk.

How does participating in the Lord's Supper somehow mysteriously nourish us (vv. 55-58)?

11. Why do several of Jesus' disciples decide to turn away and not follow him any longer (vv. 60, 66)?

12. How might we guard ourselves against the temptation to turn away from Jesus in the face of his often difficult and demanding words to us?

PRAY

Verse 34 can be used to this day, as it stands, as the prayer that we all need to pray if our deepest needs are to be met: "Master, give us this bread—give it to us always!" Amen.

DISPUTES ABOUT JESUS

John 7:1-52

Y ou'll find out how when you really want to."

Jeff's mother was trying, not for the first time, to teach him how to cook. He just couldn't get the hang of it. He would see what she was doing and copy her, but when he tried later to do it himself, he would do things in the wrong order, forget vital ingredients or leave things burning on the stove. His heart just wasn't in it.

"Well," repeated his mother, "one of these days you'll have to do it for yourself, and then you'll learn soon enough."

The same is true in several areas of life. The teenage girl who hates learning a foreign language suddenly becomes keen on it when, on holiday abroad, she meets an attractive young man who doesn't speak much of her language. The fellow who's never bothered to learn to swim suddenly wants to when all his friends are going sailing and tell him he must learn to swim if he's going to feel safe on the boat.

As so often, these illustrations point toward what Jesus is saying without exhausting its significance. If anyone wants to do God's will, they will know whether the teaching which Jesus is giving comes from God, or whether he's just making it up to boost his own position and reputation. If, that is, somebody really intends to do God's will when they discover it, then it will become clear to them that Jesus really is from God.

OPEN

What motivates you to learn something new? Give an example.

STUDY

1. *Read John 7:1-18.* Many Jewish communities around the world keep the festival of Tabernacles, or "Booths," to this day. The "tabernacles" in question are usually makeshift shelters, made out of whatever comes to hand, set up in the open air in a back yard or porch. Their purpose, like so many Jewish traditions, is to remind the people of the time when their ancestors wandered in the wilderness, living in tents, that is, tabernacles or booths. The festival, like the Passover, was regarded as a key symbol of the great national hope: the coming of the Messiah, and liberation from Rome.

   What reason does Jesus give his brothers for not wanting to go up to Jerusalem and show himself to the world at the festival of Tabernacles (vv. 6-8)?

2. How could the festival crowds have interpreted Jesus' actions had he done what his brothers urged him to do?

3. The contrast between Jesus and his brothers is seen in terms of their different attitudes toward "the world." At one level, "the world" means the whole created universe, including all the peoples of the earth (v. 4). But at another level it means the deep-seated attitude that turns away from the loving Creator and tries to organize its life independently of him (v. 7).

   How are we sometimes deceived into living and acting according to the principles of "the world" rather than the radically different way that Jesus demonstrates?

4. What "considerable dispute" about Jesus was going on among the people at the feast (v. 12)?

5. A central clue to this passage is verse 17: if anyone wants to do God's will, they will know whether the teaching which Jesus gives comes from God, or whether he's just making it up to boost his own position or reputation.

   What does this imply about the Judeans—the religious leaders—in this passage?

6. Jesus was not trying to boost his own reputation, but God's (v. 18). How might we follow Jesus' example in this as we seek to speak the truth in our own day?

7. *Read John 7:19-52.* What are the two radically different attitudes to the law of Moses that Jesus highlights in verses 21-24?

8. What is Jesus trying to communicate about the ultimate purpose of the law?

9. Some first-century Jews believed the Messiah would appear mysteri- ously, with nobody knowing where he came from (v. 27). Jesus' reply is not what we expect. Instead of saying, "Ah, but you don't know where I *really* come from" (meaning, from God), he agrees that they know where his hometown is. He then turns the question around. While insisting they are indeed ignorant of something, their real ig- norance is not so much about him, Jesus, but about God. So naturally they cannot associate the Jesus they are seeing with the true God.

   The same challenge comes to today's world. Often people look at Jesus and draw conclusions about him based on faulty ideas of God and the world. But the Christian message insists that people must learn afresh who God is, what the world is and who we ourselves are, by looking at Jesus.

In what ways has the Jesus you've encountered so far in John's Gospel challenged the way you understand God, yourself and the world?

10. What bold invitation and promise does Jesus offer to people in verses 37-38?

John is careful to tell us that Jesus is making this invitation on the last day of the festival of Tabernacles, which had among its celebratory rituals a moment when the priests would pour out water and wine around the altar. Among the prayers that were regularly prayed at the festival were prayers for rain and for the resurrection of the dead; so the theme not only of water but also of new life were spot on for the subjects that would be in people's minds.

11. Servants of the priests were sent to arrest Jesus (v. 32) but they return without having done the job (vv. 44-45). What excuse do they give and how do the Pharisees respond?

12. What then is ironic about the question Nicodemus asks the Pharisees?

13. John's Gospel portrays a wide variety of responses to Jesus, just as there are today. How do you respond to the different ideas people have about Jesus today?

PRAY

Give thanks to God for the rivers of living water that even today overflow in our hearts by the Spirit he has sent us. Pray that you will be one who genuinely seeks to do God's will and are thus able to recognize him and know him as he really is—without pride or idolatry getting in the way.

NOTE ON JOHN 7:5

Jesus' brothers seem to be half believing and half not. They see that he's doing remarkable things, but they don't "believe" in the full sense that John is talking about. They see Jesus as an extraordinary wonder-worker—one who might gain a larger following if only he would appear on a larger stage. But they have no sense that his mission will involve a single, final, decisive action through which Israel and the world will be changed for good.

NOTE ON JOHN 7:41-42

This is the only time in John's Gospel that either Bethlehem or David is mentioned, though John almost certainly knew the traditions which we find in Matthew and Luke, according to which Jesus was born in Bethlehem, though spending most of his early years in Galilee. It may be that here already John intends that his readers, whom he expects to know those stories or others like them, will recognize the irony John intends. That is, those who raise the issue of Jesus' heritage don't seem to realize they are actually speaking accurately about where Jesus came from.

NOTE ON JOHN 7:52

The Pharisees further show their ignorance of Scripture in that both the prophets Jonah and Hosea came from Galilee. And when John has them say that no prophet "rises up" or "arises" from Galilee, the word he uses is almost always used elsewhere in the book to refer to the resurrection. Jonah was proverbial for coming, so it seemed, back "from the dead" after three days in the belly of the fish; and Hosea contains the prophecy that God will "raise us up on the third day" (Hosea 6:2).

THE LIGHT OF THE WORLD

John 7:53—8:29

The house is on fire! Get up at once!"

She burst into the dormitory where several of the other girls were sleeping. She dashed to the nearest bed and shook the sleeper violently.

"Come on! There's no time! You'll be burnt alive!"

"Go back to sleep!" came the reply. "It's just one of your stupid nightmares! Stop making a nuisance of yourself!"

"Well, I'm going out right now!" she said. "And if you don't come with me you'll be fried in your beds!"

In this passage, Jesus is offering his contemporaries a last chance to change, to trust him, to act on his warnings, and so to escape the fate that is otherwise going to come on them.

OPEN

What would be your reaction to someone shouting at you in the middle of the night? What difference would it make who was doing the shouting?

STUDY

1. *Read John 7:53—8:11.* There is a puzzle about this story. It doesn't really seem to fit here. The earliest copies of John's Gospel do in fact run straight from 7:52 to 8:12, leaving this story out altogether. At the same time, some manuscripts put it in, but in a different place.

   How well do you think this story fits into John's Gospel at this point?

2. Whether or not the story of the woman and her accusers originally belonged here, it certainly helps us understand the chapter which it now introduces as the anger and opposition to Jesus increases. This chapter as it now stands begins with people wanting to stone a woman to death; it ends with them wanting to stone Jesus (8:59).

   How does Jesus avoid the trap set for him?

3. What does his response imply about the law? about God?

4. How does Jesus in effect put himself in the firing line from which he has just rescued the woman?

5. Since we are not told, we can only imagine how Jesus' declaration of forgiveness changed the woman's life. In what ways does intentionally living each day by the forgiveness Jesus gives change our lives?

6. *Read John 8:12-29.* The Pharisees seem to think this is a pretrial hearing against Jesus. How does Jesus put them on trial instead?

7. Why do the Judeans fail to understand what he means?

8. Jesus tells the Jewish leaders he is the light of the world. Why can light be both a threat and a benefit?

The idea of God calling someone to be the means of bringing light to the world is rooted in ancient Judaism. There, in the prophet Isaiah in particular, it is Israel who will be the world's true light. But, ultimately, it is the Lord's servant who is anointed to bring God's truth and justice to the world, and who at the climax of the book dies a cruel death to achieve the goal (Isaiah 42:6; 49:6; 53:1-12; 60:1, 3). The claim to be the world's true light, like so much Jesus says in this Gospel, is not in itself a claim to be divine (though John believes that, and wants us to believe it too); it is a claim to be Israel's Messiah.

9. What do the Judeans think Jesus is talking about when he says he is
    "going away" (8:22)?

10. Why is it ironic that they are unable to understand how Jesus will
    really die?

11. When we read a sentence like "you will die in your sin," most of us
    imagine that it refers only to an inward, spiritual condition, a spirit-
    ual death that takes place inside the heart and soul. It is a spiritual
    death that takes place at, or after, physical death for those who have
    turned their backs on God.

    But in the other Gospels we can see that Jesus' warnings also have
    a more specific reference, to events that were taking place in his own
    day, to the great crisis and devastation that was building up in the
    Middle East. Echoes of this find their way into John as well: in chapter
    11, Caiaphas warns his fellow leaders that if they're not careful, the
    Romans will come destroy the holy city altogether. That's the threat
    that hangs over Jesus' contemporaries; they know it and so does he.

    What alternative does Jesus offer those who are threatened by this
    crisis?

12. When there's a crisis, nettles have to be grasped, difficult decisions have to be made, opponents have to be confronted.

In what way is our world in need of the same kind of urgent message Jesus delivered to the Judeans in his day?

PRAY

Reflect on the urgency of believing in Jesus in the midst of this dark world, thanking God for the true Light that shines in the darkness. Ask God to give you boldness to live and speak in such a way that communicates this urgency to those around you with love and compassion, just as Jesus did.

12

THE TRUTH
WILL MAKE YOU FREE

John 8:30-59

The square was crowded. Indeed, it was more than crowded: it was packed to overflowing. People were leaning from windows in the beautifully sculpted office blocks around the square. It was lunchtime, but nobody was thinking of eating. There must have been at least a hundred thousand people in all, and they were all singing.

I remember it vividly. It was the first time I'd ever been in such a crowd. It was in Nathan Phillips Square in the heart of Toronto, and it was April 5, 1968—the day after Martin Luther King Jr. had been assassinated. As far as I remember, the demonstration wasn't organized; it just happened. And everyone was singing, "We Shall Overcome."

We sang it a lot in those days. It became a sort of anthem of the black liberation movement, but it went wider too. It was part of the 1960s sea change in which many of us who had grown up after the Second World War began to ask why so much was still so wrong. It had—as Martin Luther King Jr. would have wanted to give it—a specifically biblical and Christian message. Freedom was part of what the gospel had promised. It wasn't just a promise for freedom from this world, for a new life after death. It was a promise about freedom in the here and now.

OPEN

Have you ever been part of a large crowd gathered together for a common purpose? What stands out to you about that experience?

STUDY

1. *Read John 8:30-59.* How do the Judeans respond to Jesus' statement that the truth will make them "free" (vv. 32-33)?

2. Why do they react so strongly?

3. Jesus doesn't point out, as he might have done, that the foundation of their national life and faith was not just Abraham, but the exodus which had taken place after their slavery in Egypt. He goes straight to the heart of what he means. There is a worse slavery than that which they had suffered in Egypt, or the semislavery they were suffering under the rule of Rome. It was a slavery to sin.

   How does sin enslave?

4. What is the truth that Jesus is talking about that will set them free?

5. The charge that Jesus is putting to his contemporaries is that they are confusing two sets of family membership: being children of

Abraham and being children of God. They have been assuming that being children of Abraham automatically means being children of God, but John the Baptist, Jesus and the early Christians insisted this wasn't so. In fact, they insisted that the children of Abraham had been deeply and seriously affected by the disease of sin, the disease of which the rest of the human race was already suffering. The same is true today, not least when people assume that nominal membership of a Christian church means they are automatically in God's favor.

What happens if the people called to carry Jesus' light into the world are themselves infected with the darkness?

6. What charges does Jesus speak against the Jews of his day in verses 37-47?

7. What evidence led Jesus to make these charges?

8. However we imagine the devil, it is clear that there is a force which opposes God and his good creation, which drives people to acts of destruction and murder, and which regularly invents lies—the "religious" ones are often the most effective—to excuse such action and to even make it appear noble and right.

What "religious" lies today does the devil convince the church of to excuse destructive or even violent actions?

9. Why do Jesus' adversaries accuse him of having a demon (v. 48)?

10. Jesus could have answered the question of verse 53 by simply saying that God gives life to the faithful departed—a life with him in the present, and a newly embodied life in the resurrection to come (see 5:25-29), as most Jews of the time believed. But he doesn't. He goes further, claiming in verses 54-56 that the one true God is at work in and through him, and that Abraham himself, in trusting this one God and his promises for the future, had celebrated the fact that he would see the day of Jesus.

This seems to mean that Abraham, in trusting God's promises that through his family all the peoples of the earth would be blessed, was actually looking ahead to the day when Jesus would bring that promise into reality. He was claiming that he, Jesus, is at last embodying what the one living God, Abraham's God, had envisaged and promised all those years ago.

What does Jesus mean in the crucial verse 58 when he says, "Before Abraham existed, I Am"?

11. Why does this provoke such an extreme response (v. 59)?

12. In what ways do people in our own day still respond with confusion or even anger to the kinds of claims Jesus makes for himself in this chapter?

PRAY

Ask God to deliver you each day from the lies and delusions of the devil, thanking him that the opposite of these lies is the one Truth that makes you—and all who would trust in him—genuinely free.

13

THE MAN BORN BLIND

John 9

The streetlights weren't working properly that night as my friend walked home late from work. As he took the shortcut through the alley-way toward his own street, it was almost pitch dark. He knew the path well enough and wasn't worried about it.

But a moment later he paused. He'd heard a small noise in the darkness just ahead of him. He waited and listened; but, hearing no more, he guessed he'd been mistaken and started to walk on. At once he heard the noise again. Again he stopped, and felt a small shiver of fear. What was it? Who was it?

He decided to put on a brave face. "Who's that?" he asked, hoping his voice didn't sound either too fearful or too threatening.

"Is that you, Peter?" asked the voice of a neighbor. "Thank goodness! I couldn't see who it was and I was scared stiff!"

Their eyes grew used to the dark and they laughed together. They had both been afraid of each other, quite needlessly.

What we have in this passage is the two-way power of fear, acted out as the Pharisees, and the parents of a man born blind, try to come to terms with someone who could now see for the first time.

OPEN

Have you ever been spooked by something in the darkness? Was there a real need to be afraid?

STUDY

1. *Read John 9:1-41.* What does the disciples' question in verse 2 reveal about their beliefs about people born with disabilities?

2. How does Jesus correct their understanding and simultaneously reveal more about his work in the world (vv. 3-5)?

3. How does this affect the way you think about people in your life who are disabled or handicapped in some way?

At the start of the book of Genesis, God was faced with chaos. He didn't waste time describing the chaos, analyzing it or discussing whose fault it was. Instead, he created light; and, following the light, a whole new world. So here, John wants us to understand, Jesus "is doing the works of the one who sent him." A new chaos is on the way—the "night," the darkness, when Jesus will be killed and the world will seem to plunge back into primal confusion. But at the moment he is establishing the new world of light and healing. After the chaos of Good Friday and Holy Saturday, he will bring the new creation itself into being with the light of the first Easter Day (John 20:1).

4. Why did the Judeans seek out the parents of the blind man (vv. 18-19)?

5. The synagogue was the focus of the whole community. If you were put out of the synagogue, you'd probably be better off leaving the area altogether. The man's parents are afraid, because they know the threat against anyone saying Jesus is the Messiah. They are anxious for their social standing, their livelihood, perhaps their lives.

    How does the way the blind man's parents respond to the Judeans reflect this fear?

6. Describe fears you've had about speaking plainly regarding your beliefs about Jesus because of the social consequences.

7. What argument does the blind man use to defend that Jesus is from God (vv. 30-33)?

8. Why do the Judeans respond by throwing him out of the synagogue (v. 34)?

9. The work of bringing God's judgment to bear on the world, of setting things right, was often regarded by Jewish thinkers as the proper work of the Messiah, the one who would come into the world from God. One of the great messianic pictures of the time, drawn from the book of Daniel, is that of the "son of man," who is exalted to a seat alongside God and given the task of bringing God's judgment to the world. So when Jesus finds the man who had been healed—and who has now been thrown out of the synagogue—and asks him whether he believes in the son of man, this is what Jesus means. How does the man respond to this question (vv. 36, 38)?

10. What progression of belief do you see in the man through this chapter?

11. Why do you think the man believes while the Pharisees remain unbelieving?

12. How is verse 41 a complete reversal of where the chapter began?

13. Being a Christian is often confusing. People try to interpret your experience for you, to put you in this or that category, to label you. Often this is so they don't have to take you quite seriously. What you must do is stick to what you know. "I used to be blind; now I can see."

In what way is sticking to this simple truth costly, but ultimately not as costly as denying what, in Jesus, God has truly done for you?

PRAY

Give thanks to God for the light and healing he has brought to a dark and hurting world through Jesus. Pray that you will never be blinded by what you think you can see clearly, but that you would always be eager for the kind of sight only Jesus can give.

THE GOOD SHEPHERD

John 10

We stood on the cliffs and watched as the mother birds swooped in from the sea with mouthfuls of fish. There, below us, were thousands of young birds, all waiting eagerly, all screaming their peculiar cry. They were all jostling and pushing, falling over and scrambling about. Somehow, unerringly, the mothers picked out the single voice of their own chick from the teeming, noisy crowd. It seemed like a miracle.

I suppose we shouldn't be too surprised. Perhaps all human voices sound alike to birds—yet a father or mother will recognize their child's voice in a crowded room. But those of us who don't have much to do with the bird or animal kingdoms on a daily basis are often startled at just how much animals can distinguish between different people as well as between members of their own species. To this day, in the Middle East, a shepherd will go into a crowded sheepfold and call out his own sheep one by one, naming them. They will recognize his voice and come to him.

OPEN

Have you ever been able to instantly recognize the voice of a loved one in the midst of a noisy crowd? Describe the situation.

STUDY

1. *Read John 10:1-18.* What contrasts does Jesus set up in his opening parable in verses 1-5?

2. The promise of full life, "full to overflowing" (v. 10), is as relevant for us today as it was then. The modern Western world has discovered how unsatisfying materialism really is, and is looking for something more, something beyond. Many thieves have told lies, and have deceived the sheep, stolen them and left them for dead.

   How might we—as Jesus' sheep—learn to be more attentive to his voice and less easily deceived by those who seek to harm us?

3. What distinguishing mark of the "good shepherd" does Jesus repeat three times in verses 11-18?

4. The original "sheep" are the people of Israel. Jesus is calling them, and those from among his Jewish contemporaries who are ready for the call are hearing his voice, trusting him and coming to him. But, as Israel's prophets and wise writers had always hinted, the God of Israel was never interested *only* in Israel. His call to Israel was for the sake of the whole world. The "other sheep" (v. 16) are that great company, from every nation under heaven, that God intends to save, and save through Jesus. The Jewish Messiah is to become the Lord,

the shepherd of the whole world. So the Gentiles were no longer the enemy. They are sheep who have not yet been brought into the sheepfold.

How might this announcement have sounded in a world—Jesus' own world—run by Rome?

5. How does Jesus' desire to open wide the sheepfold for all who would hear his voice challenge some of our "ways of doing church" today?

The father loves the shepherd, especially because he will express the father's own love for the world by giving up his life for it. If he does this in obedience to the father's will, he will also receive it back again (v. 18); Jesus here makes the Jewish hope of general resurrection the personal and specific aim of his own work, anticipating the longer discussion in the next chapter.

Behind this, all through, is the ancient prophecy in Ezekiel 34. There's a strange thing in that chapter. Sometimes the prophet speaks of God becoming the true shepherd of Israel. But then, later, he speaks of David—in other words, of the Messiah—as the true shepherd, with God being God over shepherd and sheep alike. "Well, which is it?" we want to ask Ezekiel. He doesn't answer. He just points into the future. Only in this chapter of John do we see how it all fits together. As Jesus will finally say in verse 30, "I and the father are one." God is the shepherd; the king is the shepherd. It makes sense in Jesus and nowhere else.

6. *Read John 10:19-42.* What was the crowd's split reaction to Jesus' teaching about the shepherd and the sheep, and his claim about his relationship with the father (vv. 20-21)?

7. In what specific ways—that we've seen throughout John's Gospel— has Jesus already clearly told the people whether or not he is the Messiah (v. 25)?

8. It is interesting to observe that where people have become unclear on Jesus' close relation to the father, they have often become unclear also on the certainty of Christian hope, and vice versa. Those who hear Jesus' voice and recognize it as the voice of "their" shepherd will be safe forever. He will look after them, and even death itself, the last great enemy, cannot ultimately harm them. The reason Jesus can be so confident of this is that the guarantee is his own unbreak- able bond of love and union with the father, and the fact that the "sheep" he owns are the ones the father has given him.

   In what way does this truth enable us to live our lives as Christians with confidence?

9. Why do the Judeans pick up stones to stone Jesus (vv. 31-33)?

10. In verse 34, Jesus quotes a Bible verse that has puzzled many people. It comes from Psalm 82. God himself is speaking, addressing Israel at Mount Sinai, reminding them that when the law arrived through Moses, they were given a noble, superhuman status simply by receiving it. The unity of the divine and human had arrived in their midst. But God goes on to warn them that they haven't lived up to it, and so will be punished.

    What do you think Jesus was trying to say by quoting this passage to the Judeans who stood there ready to kill him?

11. If the religious leaders in Jerusalem had difficulty with Jesus' claim, even the country folk in the land beyond the Jordan could draw the right conclusions. They, after all, had nothing to lose. The question we have to face today is whether we are ready to look at Jesus with that open, vulnerable gaze, and to draw the right conclusion for ourselves.

    What kinds of concerns or anxieties keep us from looking fully at Jesus and believing in all that he is for us?

PRAY

Give thanks to God for sending the sacrificial Shepherd to lay down his life for you and the whole world. Ask that you would always be attentive to his voice, and that you'd always be able to distinguish it from the thieves and liars who seek your destruction.

NOTE ON JOHN 10

When we think of leaders, we think of people running big corporations—presidents and prime ministers. In the Bible the ideal king is pictured as a shepherd (Ezekiel 34), perhaps modeled on the shepherd-boy David, who became the king after God's own heart. In a world where they knew about the intimate contact and trust between shepherd and sheep, this was their preferred way of talking about kingship.

In verses 7-10 Jesus highlights the role of shepherd as a gate. In many Eastern sheepfolds, the shepherd lies down at night in the gateway, to stop the sheep getting out and to stop predators getting in. The emphasis is on the safety, and the fulfilled life, of the sheep.

THE RAISING OF LAZARUS

John 11

A friend of mine had been invited to take on the leadership of a vibrant, growing church. He and his family were eager to go and meet this new challenge. But the church authorities seemed to be dragging their feet about where he was going to live.

Meanwhile suitable houses near the church were on the market, and nothing was being done. My friend and his family prayed about it, and still nothing happened. I and others prayed about it, wrote letters, made phone calls, and still nothing happened. The time came for him to be installed at the church; it was a great occasion, but still nothing definite had happened.

Finally, as the whole church prayed about what was to be done, the logjam burst. The decision was made. And one of the most suitable houses, which they had looked at from the beginning, had now come down in price. The church authorities bought it, the family moved in and the new ministry began. But I shan't forget the months of frustration, during which it seemed as though nothing was happening.

God doesn't play games with us. Of that I am quite sure. And yet his ways are not our ways. His timing is not our timing. One of the most striking reminders of this comes in the present passage.

OPEN

Have you ever been frustrated by the feeling that something important needs to happen and yet nothing seems to be happening? How did the situation turn out?

STUDY

1. *Read John 11:1-37.* What is Jesus' response when he first hears that Lazarus is sick?

2. This opening section (vv. 1-16) is about the ways in which Jesus surprises people and overturns their expectations. How does Jesus do this in these verses?

3. In what ways has Jesus surprised you and overturned your expectations of what it means to follow him?

4. Jesus tells them a strange little saying that people that walk in the daytime don't trip up, but people who walk around in darkness do (vv. 9-10). What point was Jesus trying to make?

5. What is the first thing Martha says to Jesus when he finally arrives
    in Bethany?

6. Martha had to hurry off to meet Jesus and confront him directly.
    Many of us are like that. We must tell Jesus what we think of him
    and his strange ways. What "if only" do you have that you need to
    take to Jesus, openly expressing your frustration with him, just as
    Martha did?

Instead of looking at the past, and dreaming about what might have
been (but now can't be), Jesus invites Martha to look to the future.
"Your brother will rise again." She knows, as well as Jesus does, that
this is standard Jewish teaching. They shared the vision of Isaiah 65
and 66: a vision of the new heavens and new earth. God's whole new
world, a world like ours only with its beauty and power enhanced and
its pain, ugliness and grief abolished. Within that new world, they
believed, all God's people from ancient times to the present would be
given new bodies, to share and relish the life of the new creation.

Martha believes this, but her rather flat response in verse 24
shows that it isn't at the moment very comforting. But she isn't prepared for Jesus' response. The future has burst into the present. The
new creation, and with it the resurrection, has come forward from
the end of time into the middle of time. "I am the resurrection and
the life," he says. "Resurrection" isn't just a doctrine. It isn't just a
future fact. It's a *person,* and here he is standing in front of Martha,
teasing her to make the huge jump of trust and hope.

7. Jesus bursts into tears at the moment he sees Mary, and all the Judeans with her, in tears (vv. 33-35). The Word, through whom the worlds were made, weeps like a baby at the grave of his friend. Only when we stop and ponder this will we understand the full mystery of John's Gospel.

   How does this challenge the way people—including many Christians—often understand God?

8. *Read John 11:38-57.* We cannot but connect these two: the fate of Lazarus and the fate of Jesus. We cannot but suppose that Jesus, in praying for Lazarus and then raising him to life, was aware that he was walking toward his own death, and praying his way into the Father's will as to what would happen thereafter.

   What are some similarities you notice between the story of the raising of Lazarus and that of Jesus' own resurrection?

9. What major differences do you see between these stories?

10. We should remember that in this story the unspoken clue to it all was prayer and faith. If Jesus needed to spend time praying and waiting, how much more will we. What areas of your life right now most require prayer and patient waiting on the Lord to demonstrate his power?

11. What seems to be the biggest fear among the chief priests and the Pharisees when they hear of the sign Jesus has performed in raising Lazarus (v. 48)?

12. The authorities are naturally jumpy. They know plenty of revolutionary movements in recent times, many of which had begun, as Jesus' movement had, in Galilee. They know that they all come to the same thing in the end if the Romans would call up their troops. Indeed, many of the Pharisees themselves, and perhaps some of the priests too, longed to see Roman rule thrown off. They knew the way their people's minds worked. But though many Jewish leaders longed to be free from this threat of Roman destruction, free to order their national life without having to do what Rome said, they greatly preferred the semi-freedom that Rome granted them to the devastation that would follow if a major revolution sprang up.

How does Caiaphas unknowingly summarize in his comment in verse 50 both a cynical political perspective and Jesus' own vocation to protect the sheep?

13. Jesus' movement is different from all the revolutionary movements that came before or after. How is Jesus' movement still different from any of the other options we ourselves might choose to live for in our own day?

PRAY

Approach Jesus with your grief and frustration just as Martha did, pray urgently to him, and then listen for the way he cries and bears this pain along with you. Pray that you may trust wholly in the one who is the resurrection and the life and wait patiently for him to come and call you forth into his wonderful resurrection life as well.

NOTE ON JOHN 11:48

The mention of the Romans in this passage (which happens to be the first and only time in all four gospels where the word *Romans* is mentioned) explains a lot. By evoking the whole Roman world that stands behind the gospels, it helps us understand why people had the anxieties they did—both ordinary Jews and their leaders. The Romans had taken over most of the Middle East about a century before. There weren't many Roman soldiers about in ordinary towns and villages, but there were whole legions stationed a few miles north, in Syria, and the governor of Judea could call on them for help at any time. That had happened in living memory, and thousands of young rebel Jews had been crucified when the army marched in.

The Jewish leaders clearly thought that's what would happen if Jesus went any further. Healing blind people was one thing; but raising the dead, and doing so publicly where a lot of people could scurry back to Jerusalem and tell their friends about it—this was too much. Obviously, they thought he was gathering support for some kind of prophetic or even messianic action, perhaps a march on Jerusalem itself. Once that happened, if the Romans got wind of it, they would call up the troops. And that would be the end of any national hope they might still have.

THE HOUR HAS COME

John 12

I always hate it when, in a movie or novel, a social event suddenly becomes tense and fraught. People who write novels and screenplays seem to like them: anger and bitterness bubbling to the surface, family members losing their tempers with each other, and guests looking on in dismay at the collapse of the occasion. For a dramatist, of course, such moments enable all sorts of useful points to be made. The plot can take a new turn. But they make me shudder. A shared meal ought to be a time of support and friendship, not of destruction and violence.

Part of the tragedy of this opening scene in John 12 is that Jesus badly needs and wants his followers to be united at this moment. The rest of the world is plotting against him; his friends might at least have the decency, you might suppose, to stick together and back him! But no. We can feel the tension crackling in the air.

OPEN

Have you ever experienced a shared meal or social function that turned ugly with tension and strife? How did you respond?

STUDY

1. *Read John 12:1-26.* What contrast do we see between Martha and Mary in verses 2-3?

2. Mary steals center stage by her apparently outrageous gesture of anointing Jesus' feet and wiping them with her hair. She would need to let it down for the purpose; that's roughly the equivalent, at a modern polite dinner party, of a woman hitching up a long skirt to the top of her thighs.

   What do you think motivated Mary to behave in such an extreme way?

3. There is no escaping the challenge posed by the standoff between Mary and Judas—extravagant wastefulness versus prudent caution. And then there's Martha's faithful, almost unnoticed service. Put aside your natural inclination to distance yourself from Judas and answer this question: Where are *you* in this picture? Which character—Mary, Martha or Judas—do you identify with and why?

4. Why did the chief priests begin planning to kill Lazarus too (vv. 9-11)?

5. Although it's the wrong time of year, the symbols of Jesus' entry into Jerusalem go with Hanukkah—which John has already mentioned in 10:22. When Judas Maccabaeus defeated the pagan invaders and cleansed the temple in 164 B.C., his followers entered the city waving palm branches in celebration (1 Maccabees 13:51; 2 Maccabees 10:7). Now, even though it's in the spring, not mid-winter when Hanukkah is celebrated, Jesus' followers wave palm branches to welcome him.

   We don't have to look far to find out why. Hanukkah was when Judas and his family became kings of Israel. Jesus and his followers were, so to speak, bringing together Hanukkah and Passover. They were saying both that Jesus was the true king, come to claim his throne, and that this was the moment when God would set Israel free once and for all. The ride on the donkey, with its echo of Zechariah 9:9, makes the same point. And John adds other echoes of prophecies and psalms which all point in the same direction. Jesus is the true king, coming at last to set his people free.

   What tone of voice do you think the Pharisees used and what were they suggesting when they said, "Look—the world has gone after him" (v. 19)?

6. Immediately following the Pharisees' statement in verse 19 some foreigners approach the disciples, wanting to see Jesus (vv. 20-23). What does John want us to see in connecting these two events?

7. Jesus tells his mother in John 2:4 that his time has not yet come. John makes a similar comment in 7:30. Now, in 12:23, he says the

time has come. What is the time that has come and how does that connect to Jesus' comments about a seed being planted and dying?

8. What does Jesus say that has to do with those who would follow him?

9. *Read John 12:27-50.* The Word that had become flesh, the one in whom the Father's own love and power were truly seen, the one who healed the sick, turned water into wine, opened blind eyes and raised Lazarus to life: he was troubled. Deeply troubled. Troubled right down in his heart (v. 27).

   Jesus' picture of God was big enough that he could still have a troubled spirit. What hints are there in verses 27-36 that suggest how our understanding of God can still allow us to also have emotions such as these?

10. John has been telling us the story of new creation. The "signs" have been building up: water into wine in chapter 2, the nobleman's son in chapter 4, the healing of the cripple in chapter 5, the bread in the desert in chapter 6, the man born blind in chapter 9 and most recently the raising of Lazarus in chapter 11. And John has hinted, and will say again later (20:30), that Jesus did many, many other "signs" as well. These six are just the tip of the iceberg, selected to

make their individual points about new creation, new dimensions to God's work, new exodus, new life, new light. And yet . . . though he had done all these things, they still didn't believe.

Pharaoh refused to believe despite the powerful signs Moses produced in Exodus 8—12. Similarly, to what does John, recalling words from Isaiah (53:1 and 6:10), attribute the people's continued lack of belief (vv. 37-41)?

11. Why don't the few rulers who do believe in Jesus speak up about their faith (vv. 42-43)?

12. In John 12:44-50 Jesus speaks to the crowds in Jerusalem for the last time. The next time they see him it will be as a prisoner, standing before Pilate. He will be on trial, and his words will be sifted as evidence against him. How do you respond to the stupendous claims Jesus makes here?

PRAY

Give thanks to God that in the death and resurrection of Jesus, the dark ruler of this world was overthrown and the new creation was born. Ask that God would give you a heart that truly believes in Jesus and is courageous enough to say so in the presence of others who might not understand or support your faith.

WASHING THE
DISCIPLES' FEET

John 13

I was given a beautiful present this week. To celebrate a special anniversary, someone close to me spent hours and hours weaving a careful tapestry, a needlepoint work of art. The theme comes from one of the early Celtic Gospels, and is a picture of the four Gospel writers, Matthew, Mark, Luke and John. Each one is accompanied by the particular symbol some early Christians gave them: Matthew by an angel, Mark by a lion, Luke by an ox and John by an eagle.

I've never done a needlepoint tapestry like that, but I've watched, and I know how it's done. You need the pattern, the outline: someone has to design it, and color it on to the canvas so that the artist can see which color threads go where. Then the pattern has to be followed very carefully, stitch by stitch. It's laborious, and a bit of a strain on the eyes, but as the work develops there is a growing sense of excitement as the picture comes alive, and of anticipation of the complete work. Finally it is framed, ready to be hung on the wall as an object of beauty and interest, a sign (in this case) both of love and of a particular moment.

Likewise in John 13 Jesus speaks of giving his followers a pattern to copy.

OPEN

Have you ever done a craft or project that required you to follow a very strict pattern? What did you find difficult about the process? What did you find enjoyable or rewarding?

STUDY

1. *Read John 13:1-20.* What was Simon Peter's initial response when Jesus began to wash his feet (vv. 6, 8)?

2. How does Peter's response indicate that he has perhaps misunderstood what Jesus has been trying to communicate to his disciples about his mission and purpose?

3. The little drama with Peter is funny on the outside but deeply serious on the inside. Jesus must wash us if we are to belong to him. Yes, he has already washed us, in calling us to belong to him (John 15:3); what we need day by day is the regular washing of those parts of ourselves, our personalities and bodies, that get dusty and dirty.

   In what ways do you need Jesus to "wash your feet" today?

4. What particular lesson does Jesus seek to teach his disciples by this act of foot washing (vv. 14-15)?

5. Why is it necessary for Jesus to then go on and emphasize (to the disciples and to us) that the slave is not greater than the master, that the one who is sent is not greater than the one who sends (v. 16)?

6. The point is that, for us as for Jesus, we should be looking away from ourselves, and at the world we are supposed to be serving. Where the world's needs and our vocation meet is where we ought to be, ready to take on insignificant roles if that's what God wants, or to be publicly visible if that is our calling. And, as with Jesus, the picture of foot washing is meant to serve not only as a picture of menial tasks we may be called to perform. It also points toward the challenge that Jesus issued to Peter in the last chapter of the book, to follow Jesus all the way to the cross, to lay down life itself in the service of God and the world he came to save.

    How does Jesus' teaching and example here challenge the way we often understand our own role in serving him and the world?

7. *Read John 13:21-38.* How do the disciples react when Jesus announces that one of them will betray him (v. 22)?

8. Dipping a piece of bread in the dish and passing it to someone was a sign of special friendship. Why would Jesus use this as the sign to indicate which disciple would betray him?

9. As in 12:27, so here in 13:21, Jesus is troubled in spirit. There is no
   shame in spirit-trouble; it's what you get when you're a foot washer,
   a generous-love person, open to deep friendship and to the serious
   wounds that only friends can give.

   How might Jesus' openness to deep friendship (and hurt!) serve as a
   model for us in our own relationships?

10. After Judas departs, what new commandment does Jesus give the
    remaining disciples (v. 34)?

11. Love, of course, is central in many parts of the Old Testament. The
    book of Leviticus (19:18) commanded the Israelites to love their
    neighbors as themselves. So in what way is Jesus' commandment
    "new"?

12. This love is to be the badge that the Christian community wears be-
    fore the watching world. As we read verse 35 we are bound to cringe
    in shame at the way in which professing Christians have treated
    each other down the years. We have turned the gospel into a weapon
    of our own various cultures. We have hit each other over the head
    with it, burnt each other at the stake with it. We have defined the

"one another" so tightly that it means only "love the people who reinforce your own sense of who you are."

How can we begin to live out Jesus' command in a way that genuinely communicates to the world how much he has loved us?

PRAY

Thank God for the radical act of service Jesus performed for his disciples in the washing of their feet, and ask that he would show you what it looks like to follow his example in your life. Pray that he would help you and all Christians to love one another as he has loved you so that the world might come to believe in Christ and know his deep love and friendship.

NOTE ON JOHN 13:27

John does not, I think, mean that Judas became "demon-possessed" in the same way as those unfortunate characters we meet from time to time in the other Gospels. The word "satan" in Hebrew means "accuser"; it's a legal term for someone who brings a prosecution, a charge, against someone else. What we are now to witness is Judas being used by the forces of darkness to bring a charge against Jesus, the messenger of the light. The confrontation between light and darkness, which has been hanging over the Gospel story ever since the prologue (1:5), is coming to its climax. And Judas has been willingly enlisted among the forces of darkness. The end of verse 30 is one of John's master touches as a storyteller. The door opens onto the dark night, in every sense and at every level, and Judas disappears into it.

ANOTHER HELPER

John 14

Are you sure there'll be room for us all?"

We were on our way back to a friend's house. There were two carloads of us, relaxed and happy after a football match which we'd won. The match had been at another school several miles away, and rather than going back to our own school, and from there to our homes, we'd arranged that we would stay with one member of the team who lived much closer to where the game had been played.

"I told you, didn't I?" he said. "You'll see. There's plenty of room for you all."

We had been imagining he lived in an ordinary house on an ordinary street. Even with an extension built on the back, as some of our friends had, ordinary houses only had four bedrooms, or five at the most. Were we all going to sleep on the living-room floor? What would his parents say? We turned into his driveway, and then we realized. This wasn't an ordinary street, and it wasn't an ordinary house. It was a mansion.

He grinned, a bit shyly. "Told you there would be room, didn't I?" We tumbled out and he took us upstairs. Long corridors, lots of rooms. We couldn't believe it. It was like a hotel. His father's house.

That's the image Jesus uses in John 14.

OPEN

Have you ever been surprised when you went to stay somewhere? How was the situation different from what you were expecting?

STUDY

1. *Read John 14:1-31.* Why does Jesus feel the need to reassure the disciples at this point (v. 1)?

2. What bold claim does Jesus make about himself in verse 6?

3. Why does this kind of claim often make people uncomfortable?

4. Though of course it's true that many Christians and churches have been arrogant in the way they have presented the gospel, the whole setting of this passage shows that such arrogance is a denial of the very truth it's claiming to present. The truth, the life, through which we know and find the way, is Jesus himself: the Jesus who washed the disciples' feet and told them to copy his example, the Jesus who was on his way to give his life as the shepherd for the sheep. Only when the church recovers the nerve to follow Jesus in his own mission and vocation will it be able to recover its nerve fully in making the claim of verse 6.

How might we proclaim and embody the significant message found in verse 6 in a way that is humble and faithful to the example Jesus set for us?

5. Who is the other helper Jesus promises that the Father will send the disciples when he's gone, and what will this helper do (vv. 16-17, 25-26)?

The word translated "counselor" or "helper" is rich and many-sided. It doesn't simply mean someone who comes to lend assistance in our various tasks. It certainly does mean that, but it means two other things as well. One word sometimes used is *comforter*. Comfort is a strange and wonderful thing. Have you ever noticed how, when someone is deeply distressed, the fact of having other people with them, hugging them and being alongside them, gives them strength for the next moment? When the Spirit is spoken of as the "comforter," this kind of extra strength to meet special need is in mind.

An equally good translation of the word is "advocate." An advocate stands up in a court of law and explains to the judge or jury how things are from his or her client's point of view. The advocate pleads the case. In the heavenly law court with God as the judge, his people can rest assured that they will be heard, that God will constantly be reminded of their plight, because the Spirit will plead on their behalf.

6. How are Christians in a better situation now as a result of the coming of this "other helper" than the disciples in Jesus' day?

7. How have you experienced or witnessed these greater works of the Spirit (v. 12) in your life or in the lives of others around you?

8. What remarkable promise about prayer does Jesus make in verses 13-14?

The all-important phrase "in my name" doesn't, of course, just mean adding "in the name of Jesus" to anything we might think of, however stupid, selfish or hurtful. The "name," after all, as in many cultures, is supposed to reveal the character.

Praying in Jesus' name, then, means that, as we get to know who Jesus is, so we find ourselves drawn into his life and love and sense of purpose. We will then begin to see what needs doing, what we should be aiming at within our sphere of possibilities and what resources we need to do it. When we then ask, it will be "in Jesus' name," and to his glory; and, through that, to the glory of the Father himself (v. 13).

9. How does this promise challenge the way that we pray?

10. What does the term *world* mean in verse 22?

11. There is a sharp distinction between the followers of Jesus and "the world." Only when that is realized can the next word be heard, which is another spectacular promise. Those who hold fast to Jesus and refuse to settle for a second-best, compromised discipleship, will find that his peace comes to them as a gift, a peace of the kind that "the world" can never give.

    Why is the world unable to give us this kind of peace?

12. How have you experienced the peace that comes with the presence of Jesus?

PRAY

Give thanks to the Father for sending Jesus to be the one way, truth and life for the whole world. Thank him too for not leaving us bereft but sending his Spirit to guide us, comfort us and plead on our behalf. Pray that you personally might know the peace of Jesus' presence by his Spirit at work in and around you.

NOTE ON JOHN 14:2

The only other time in John's gospel that Jesus has used the expression "my father's house" is in regard to the temple (2:16). The point about the temple, within the life of the people of Israel, was that it was the place where heaven and earth met. Now Jesus hints at a new city, a new world, a new "house." Heaven and earth will meet again when God renews the whole world. At that time there will be room for everyone.

THE TRUE VINE

John 15

One of the many areas in which I possess near-total incompetence is gardening . . . but I can mow a lawn. I can pick gooseberries. I can plant bulbs.

And I can prune roses. Someone told me how when I was young and I've never forgotten. In fact, I not only know *how* to do it, I even know *why* (well, more or less). A rose bush, left to itself, will get straggly and tangled, and grow in on itself. It will produce quite a lot of not-so-good roses rather than a smaller number of splendid ones. It will, quite literally, get in its own light. It needs help to grow in the right directions and to the right ends. So you prune it to stop it wasting its energy and being unproductive. You cut out, particularly, the parts of the plant that are growing inwards and getting tangled up. You encourage the shoots that are growing outwards, toward the light. You prune the rose, in other words, to help it to be its true self.

As far as I understand it, more or less the same thing works with vines.

OPEN

What has been your experience with gardening?

STUDY

1. *Read John 15:1-27.* In the picture Jesus describes in verses 1-3, what does each element—vine, gardener, branches, fruit—represent?

2. Within Jewish tradition, the vine was a picture of Israel. God brought a vine out of Egypt and planted it in the Promised Land (Psalm 80:8-18). It had been ravaged by wild animals and needed protecting and reestablishing. The vineyard of Israel, said Isaiah in chapter 5, has borne wild grapes instead of proper ones. Other prophets used the same picture.

   Read Isaiah 5:1-7 and Psalm 80:8-18. How do these passages shed light on what Jesus is saying about himself as the "true vine"?

3. Branches that decide to "go it alone," to try living without the life of the vine, soon discover their mistake. They wither and die and are good for nothing but the fire (v. 6).

   The urgent question, then, is this: How do we "remain" in him? What does this look like in practice?

4. Though it always hurts, we must be ready for the Father's pruning knife. How have you experienced the pruning work of the Father in your life?

5. What does Jesus identify as the highest form of love (v. 13)?

6. What event in particular was Jesus pointing to when he spoke of this highest form of love and of his disciples as his "friends" (v. 14)?

7. Jesus issues the command that we are to love one another, and so to remain in his love, because he has acted out, and will act out, the greatest thing that love can do. What are some practical ways that we can love others in the sacrificial way that Jesus has loved us?

8. What reasons does Jesus give for the world's hatred of his disciples (vv. 19, 21)?

9. What does Jesus mean when he says that his followers are not "from the world" (v. 19)?

10. It is scandalous but true that Christians have often persecuted other peoples and faiths. The idea that the gospel of Jesus and his love could be spread by any kind of violence would be a sort of sick joke if it weren't such a serious mistake. The loser in all such situations has

been the gospel itself. But this doesn't take away from the fact that Jesus' warnings in this section are not paranoid, even if they may sound that way to a comfortable, armchair version of Christianity. The young church certainly faced persecution from the very beginning.

Where do we see evidence of the world's hatred of Christ's followers today?

11. Those who follow Jesus will find themselves in a new situation, facing new dangers as well as opportunities. What comfort does Jesus offer to his disciples in the face of all that is to come (v. 26)?

12. How has the Spirit helped you find the words to speak about Jesus in times when you most needed this kind of help?

PRAY

Give thanks to the Father for graciously tending and caring for his vineyard—even if that means a little bit of pain for us branches! Pray that we may learn how to remain connected to the true life-giving vine and that we would never seek to exist apart from him. Thank him for the helper he has sent to us, and pray for the ears to hear and the courage to act on what he speaks to us in time of need.

THE SPIRIT AND THE WORLD

John 16

I once saw a film based on one of Charles Dickens's novels. The film was about poverty and the degrading effect it has on people. One of the most depressing scenes was in a lawyer's office, as the relatives of a man imprisoned for debt were desperately trying to bring a lawsuit to prove that he was owed a large sum of money, which should be paid and earn him release. The lawyers didn't care. Their clerks didn't care. Nobody cared. The case, written out on a fine piece of parchment, was rolled up, tied with a ribbon and left to gather dust along with dozens, hundreds, of others. Suddenly you could feel it: the cold realization that there was nothing you could do. Justice deferred is usually justice denied. And it was being deferred indefinitely.

There were many times during Israel's history when the nation as a whole found itself in the same situation. And they developed a regular way of thinking about it all, based on their unshakable belief that their God, the world's creator, was the God of justice. They imagined themselves in a law court.

OPEN

What other familiar films or novels illustrate this point about the denial of justice for the poor and underprivileged of this world?

STUDY

1. *Read John 16:1-33.* The earlier verses of this section say what has been said before, adding new emphases. What is repeated and what are some of these new emphases we find in verses 1-4?

2. Now that Jesus is going away, his followers need to know how things will be. They are bound to be sad, but they should be comforted by the arrival of the "helper," the Holy Spirit. In particular, they should take heart. In the "lawsuit" they will find themselves in (not necessarily specific occasions of being brought before courts, but the heavenly lawsuit Jesus is imagining, in which he will be pitted against "the world"), the "helper" will do the job of the advocate.

   In what ways will the Spirit—acting as the advocate—prove the world to be wrong in their assumptions and accusations regarding Jesus and his followers (vv. 8-11)?

3. In what ways do we still see the Spirit advocating on behalf of those who suffer oppression and injustice in the world today?

4. Part of the job of the Spirit, "the helper," will be to lead the disciples into all the truth (v. 13). The Spirit will remind them of what Jesus had already said to them. The Spirit will also guide them, nudging their minds and imaginations into the ways of knowing, and things to know, that Jesus would like to have said but couldn't at the time.

   How have you experienced this work of the Spirit—leading you into the truth and knowledge of Jesus?

5. What point is John trying to make by including the funny little dialogue in verses 16-19?

6. What image does Jesus use to describe what is going to happen in the days immediately ahead (vv. 20-22)?

Jesus' disciples are about to be plunged into a short, sharp and intensely painful period. Jesus will be taken away; but they will see him again. His death and resurrection are the necessary events that will lead to his "going to the father" and his "sending of the spirit." These are extraordinary, cataclysmic events, the like of which the world has never seen before. The disciples can hardly prepare properly for them; but Jesus wants to warn them anyway.

It's all happening because, with Jesus' death and resurrection, a new world—*the* new world—is indeed being born. This isn't just a matter of Jesus saying "there's trouble coming, but it will be all right afterwards." It's a matter of seeing that when we find ourselves a few chapters from now, at the foot of the cross, and then when we find ourselves after that with Mary Magdalene in the Easter garden, we shouldn't miss the significance of these events. They are not merely strange, shocking and even unique. They are the visible sign that God's new world really is coming to birth.

7. Jesus' people have instant, immediate, direct and valued access into the very presence of the living God. Why does Jesus say this is so (v. 27)?

8. How do Jesus' words about the character of the Father and his actions toward us challenge the way that God is often—even in the church—characterized?

9. How do the disciples respond to Jesus' teaching about the Father at the end of these great discourses (v. 29)?

10. Why is it crucial for the disciples to be able to glimpse at least a bit of the truth at this point?

11. The last word here isn't one of warning. It's one of good cheer. Somehow, even in the worst that is to come, the disciples can have a peace that will carry them through. The peace doesn't come from a detached, philosophical attitude. It isn't a matter of saying, "Oh well, these things happen." It isn't a shrug of the shoulders, resigning yourself to the world being a nasty place and there being nothing much you can do about it. It's a matter of standing on the ground that Jesus is going to win—indeed that he claims to have won already. "You'll have trouble in the world; but cheer up, I've overcome the world!"

    How does knowing that Jesus has overcome affect the way you view the trouble and suffering that come your way in life?

PRAY

Give thanks to the Father, Son and Spirit for the way they work together to demonstrate the greatest kind of love to us. Give thanks to the Father for his love and attentiveness to our prayers, to the Son for his sacrifice and victory, and to the Spirit for his advocacy and guidance. Pray that you will be able to take heart and find courage and hope in times of trouble because of what this God has done—and continues to do—for you.

21

JESUS PRAYS FOR HIS PEOPLE

John 17

In the newspapers recently a mother was punished by the courts. She had left her two young children entirely by themselves, while she went off for a foreign holiday with her new boyfriend. (The father, it seems, was nowhere to be found.) It is hard to believe that a mother could do such a thing. One wonders what she thought she would find when she got home. Tragically, such things happen in our world today.

But supposing she herself had had loving parents who were only too glad to look after the children while she was away! That would have made all the difference. She could have entrusted the little ones to them, safe in the knowledge that they would care for them as much as she did. One can imagine a mother in that situation giving her parents detailed instructions as to how each child should be looked after, not because she didn't trust her parents to look after them but because she did.

What Jesus now prays grows out of the fact that he is going away. He is entrusting the disciples to the father he has known and loved throughout his own earthly life, the father who, he knows, will care for them every bit as much as he has done himself.

OPEN

Have you ever entrusted someone or something to another person when you couldn't handle the responsibility? What was the experience like?

STUDY

1. *Read John 17:1-26.* The first section of this prayer is a celebration and a request. The two are closely linked. What is Jesus celebrating (v. 4) and what is he requesting (v. 5)?

2. In Jewish tradition the king, the Messiah, the son of man, was supposed to be lifted up to attain the position alongside the Father. The Messiah, say the psalms, will rule a kingdom that stretches from sea to sea, from "the River" to "the ends of the earth" (Psalm 72:8). In other words, he will have a universal dominion. "One like a son of man" will be exalted to share the throne of God himself (Daniel 7).

   When the Messiah takes his seat, exalted over the world, then the age to come will truly have begun—that "coming age" which Jewish prophets longed for, which Jewish sages taught would appear at the end of "the present age." It would be the time of new life, life with a new quality (not just quantity, going on and on forever). It would be, in our inadequate phrase "eternal life."

   This "eternal life," this life of the coming age, is not just something which people can have after their death. It isn't simply that in some future state the world will go on forever and ever and we will be part of it. The point is, rather, that this new sort of life has come to birth in the world in and through Jesus.

   How might this understanding of "eternal life" change the way we speak about the significance of our faith to those who do not yet know Jesus?

3. What particular concerns does Jesus bring before the Father regarding his disciples in verses 11-17?

4. In John "the world" doesn't mean the physical universe as such but the world insofar as it has rebelled against God. What would it look like in practical, everyday terms for Christians today to not be taken out of the world but instead to be kept from the evil one (v. 15)?

5. What do we learn from this prayer about the relationship between the Father and the Son?

6. This section of Jesus' prayer (vv. 9-19) has been used by pastors, teachers and other Christian leaders as they pray for those in their care. How could you use this prayer for yourself, your family, your friends or anyone else in your care?

7. In verse 20, Jesus is talking about *you*. And me. "Those who believe in me through their word," that is, through the word of his followers. What specifically is on Jesus' mind when he prays for you and me and all his followers in this and every generation (vv. 21-23)?

8. Why did Jesus see this as such a pressing need (v. 23; remember also 13:35)?

9. How have we as Christians today both failed and succeeded to live out this particular prayer of Jesus?

10. What are specific ways you or your Christian community could show oneness with other Christians from whom you are divided?

11. In the end, the whole prayer comes down to the love of the Father surrounding Jesus, and this same love, as a bond and badge, surrounding all Jesus' people, making him present to them and through them to the world (vv. 24-26).

    How can we more intentionally live as people through whom the world is invited into the love of the Father and the Son?

PRAY

When you make this prayer your own, when you enter into this chapter and see what happens, you are being invited to come into the heart of that intimate relation between Jesus and the Father and have it, so to speak, happen all around you. You might substitute "Jesus" where the prayer says "I," and replace "they" and "them" with "I" and "me" or perhaps with "we" and "us." Take some time to pray this prayer alongside Jesus and allow yourself to be caught up in the wonderful relationship he has with the Father, trusting and knowing that because of Jesus, that intimate relationship is yours too.

22

THE ARREST OF JESUS

John 18

I watched today as the television interviewer fired questions at a man whose main aim seemed to be to answer them all at great length without saying anything at all. On and on the interviewer went, trying angle after angle; but the man stood his ground. No, he repeated, our policy is such-and-such. Our main aim is to make sure that all the different interests of the region are balanced as best as can be. Yes, compromises will be needed (though he never said what). No, we don't intend to impose our own solution, but to help the region find its own. And so on. And so on.

The man was a special envoy to a part of the Middle East that has been under huge stress and pressure in recent days. He had gone from his home in the comfortable and affluent part of the world to represent the Western powers, or some of them, in an inhospitable and hostile land, where people spoke a different language not only with their lips but with their hearts and lives. Things were different there. If he could only keep things quiet, prevent trouble, present a good front to people back home, hope that no major disaster brewed up . . .

And of course that describes Pontius Pilate as well.

OPEN

When have you ever been frustrated with your political leaders because they seem to be playing games rather than looking out for the best interest of the people?

STUDY

1. *Read John 18:1-27.* Describe the mood, the feelings of this opening scene in verses 1-14.

2. What does Jesus do when he sees Judas and the soldiers coming toward him (vv. 4-8)?

3. Jesus' answer to the soldiers looking for him is simple and shocking: "I AM" (vv. 5-6). Previously he has said in John's Gospel, "I am the bread of life," "I am the light of the world," "I am the resurrection and the life" and "I am the way, the truth and the life." Why is Jesus' answer here so significant, and why does it cause such a reaction?

4. What motivated Peter to draw his sword (v. 10), and why was Jesus so upset by this (v. 11)?

5. How have you reacted in situations where Christ's name and character were attacked? Looking back, do you wish you had responded differently? If so, how?

6. The story of Adam in the Garden in Genesis 2 and 3 stands behind the garden of betrayal in this chapter, but things are reversed. Instead of sinful people hiding in the garden with God searching for them, now violent men come storming into the garden looking for Jesus who stands in plain sight.

   What is John trying to communicate by writing a kind of "new Genesis"?

7. In verses 15-27, what similarities and differences do you see between Jesus and Peter?

8. What motivates our desire to hide our connection with Jesus from others, while still somehow wanting to be loyal to him?

9. *Read John 18:28-40.* What vague accusation do the chief priests bring against Jesus before Pilate (v. 30)?

10. Pilate's policy seems to have revolved around two aims in particular. On the one hand, he wanted to keep things quiet in the turbulent Middle East where the local population deeply resented the occupying Roman forces. On the other hand, he seems to have taken delight in snubbing the Jewish people, and particularly their leaders. These two aims determined the way Pilate behaved throughout the following scenes. Though he was the representative of Roman "justice," that quality seems to have been interpreted, as in some other situations, with considerable flexibility. It all boiled down to pragmatism. To "what would work."

In light of this, why might Pilate have wanted someone else to decide the case the chief priests were bringing against Jesus (v. 31)?

11. In the ancient world, people knew what kings did. Kings ruled people according to their own wishes and whims. They could promote one person and demote another. They were all-powerful.

And people knew how kings became kings, too. Often the crown would pass from father to son, or to some other close male relative. But from time to time there would be a revolution. The way to the crown, for anyone not in the direct family line, was through violence.

This was so among the Jews as much as among the pagans. Judas Maccabaeus had established his dynasty, two hundred years before Jesus met Pilate, through military revolution against the Syrians, winning for the Jews their independence, and for himself and his family a royal status. Herod the Great, thirty years before Jesus was born, had defeated the Parthians, the great empire to the east, and Rome in gratitude had allowed him to become "King of the Jews," though he too had no appropriate background or pedigree. So when Pilate faces Jesus, and someone hints that the reason the chief priests have handed him over is because he thinks he's a king, Pilate no doubt saw the possibility that Jesus would lead a violent revolution to free the Jews.

How does Jesus respond when Pilate asks him if he is the "King of the Jews" (vv. 33-36)?

12. Jesus and Pilate discuss truth. What do they each mean by it (vv. 37-38)?

13. What response can and do we offer people—friends, relatives, neighbors—when they cynically scoff and ask questions similar to Pilate's in verse 38?

PRAY

As you consider this dark night on which Jesus was betrayed, denied and handed over to the authorities, give thanks to God for all that Jesus endured on your behalf. Ask him for the courage to be loyal to him in moments of fear and despair. Pray that he will show you how you might best participate in the work of the kingdom of the one true King.

23

THE KING OF THE JEWS

John 19:1-24

From our seats, high in the stands, we watched as the football match swung this way and that. Our team was doing well and scored a couple of early goals. We were delighted; surely they could hang on to a lead like that? When the opposition scored one back, with only ten minutes to go, we didn't mind too much. We were still in front, with not long to go.

But then the opposition pulled out its secret weapon and brought on a substitute, fresh and lively. He was exactly what the other side needed. He put fresh heart into their whole team. We watched, helpless, as our side struggled to cope with the new challenge. The inevitable happened. First, an equalizing goal. Then, three minutes before the end, the match winner. We trudged off home, thinking of that moment when the whole game had swung away from us.

That is the feeling we get at verse 12 in this passage. Pilate is in charge. And when he decides that he really does want to let Jesus go, we assume he is going to be able to do it. But then suddenly it all changes. The chief priests bring out their secret weapon. At that minute the game entirely swings away from Pilate.

OPEN

When have you experienced the sudden sinking feeling that things were definitely not going to turn out as you had been assuming they would?

STUDY

1. *Read John 19:1-24.* How do Pilate and the soldiers mock Jesus and his claims to kingship (vv. 2-3)?

2. In Genesis 1, God creates the heavens and the earth and places within this new world an image, a statue of himself, so the world will know who really rules. Except, of course, because of who God is, it isn't a statue made of stone or wood. It is itself a living being, like the animals but also unlike. This image is there for a purpose: so that, through this image, God can rule over his new world wisely and lovingly. And also that, in coming under the rule of this image, the creation can properly honor him, its creator.

   This image, of course, is the human race (Genesis 1:26-28). In the image of God he made them; male and female he created them. And God gave them instructions to be fruitful and multiply, and look after the Garden and the animals.

   How does this chapter demonstrate the extent to which humanity had dramatically failed to accomplish its God-given purpose in the world?

3. Within the six-day creation of Genesis 1, the human race is created on the sixth day, the Friday. The work is complete. Likewise on the sixth day of the week Jesus is tried and crucified. Why is this significant in John's Gospel?

4. "Here's the man!" (v. 5). The words hang over the whole of chapter 19 as Jesus goes to the cross. This, John is telling us, is the true image of the true God. This is what it means that Jesus, the eternal Word, became flesh and lived among us (John 1:14). Look at this man, and you'll see your living, loving, bruised and bleeding God.

   How does seeing Jesus this way impact how we understand God's presence in the midst of our own suffering?

5. Just as the chief priests realize that Pilate is wanting to let Jesus go, they pull out a trump card. Why is it so effective (v. 12)?

6. Why is it so devastating to hear "We have no king but Caesar!" (v. 15) coming from the lips of the official representatives of Judaism?

7. Pagan empire comes in various forms. It may appear as the totalitarianism which claims divinity, and hence absolute allegiance, for itself. Or it may appear as the liberal democracy which banishes

"God" from its system altogether, and then regards itself as free to carve up the world to its own advantage without moral restraint. Either way the choice becomes stark.

What would it look like for us to fully side with Jesus—silent in the middle, continuing to reflect the love of God into his muddled and tragic world—as opposed to the political maneuverings of those like Pilate and the chief priests in our world?

8. Why are the chief priests furious with Pilate about the notice he hangs above Jesus' cross (vv. 19-22)?

9. What is ironic about the notice Pilate wrote?

10. Once again we must listen to what John is telling us, as Jesus goes to his death. Remember how Caiaphas had said more than he had known when he spoke, callously, about one man dying for the people (11:49-50). Remember how Jesus had been approached by some Greeks, and how in his comment on their request he had said that when he was "lifted up from the earth" he would "draw all people to himself" (12:32). Remember how Peter had declared that *he* would lay down his life for *Jesus*, and how Jesus had gently questioned whether he'd got that idea the right way around (13:37-38).

Bring all that together, stand at the foot of the cross and look up at the notice that Pilate has written. What is John emphasizing in his description of Pilate's notice?

11. As the King, Jesus is also fulfilling the extraordinary biblical prophecies about the suffering righteous one, in whom the sufferings of Israel would come to their height, and through whose tribulation and death evil would be exhausted and the kingdom of God be born on earth.

    Read Psalm 22. How are some of the prophecies of this psalm fulfilled in Jesus' suffering and death?

12. Jesus is the fulfillment of prophecy and sacred song. He is the righteous sufferer. He is the true King. He is the one through whose shameful death the weight of Israel's sin, and behind that the sin of the whole world, is being dealt with. The King of the Jews is God's chosen representative, not merely to rule the world but to redeem it.

    How does seeing Jesus' suffering and death as part of the long-term plan of God—as evidenced through the many prophecies made and fulfilled in him—help us better understand God's radical faithfulness to us?

PRAY

Prayerfully consider how great the tragedy of human sin and depravity that we—mocking and calloused, violent and self-seeking people—would be capable of sending our true King to his death, and confess to the Lord your part, your guilt, in this horror. Then rejoice and give thanks to him that in and through this very tragedy, he was at work reconciling and redeeming all of us who were guilty, all of us who had a part in it.

24

The Death of Jesus

John 19:25-42

He came up at the end of the service and shook me warmly by the hand. "I didn't really know why I was coming here this morning," he said. "I wouldn't normally have made the effort. I'd have gone somewhere closer to home. But something made me come. And then when you said what you did in your sermon" (he mentioned something I'd said which, unknown to me, was exactly what he'd needed to help him forward at a particular point), "I knew why I was here."

Many preachers will have had that experience. And many of us too know the moment when a strange compulsion makes us go to a place where, though we couldn't have known it, someone we needed to see was waiting. It's only when you look back, sometimes over a long period, that you notice these patterns and realize that, despite the horrors and tragedies of life, God is quietly working his purposes out.

The young man at the foot of the cross must have asked himself a thousand times why it had to happen. He must have asked himself many times why he had to be there. Why couldn't he have stayed in hiding like the others? Why did he have to see this horror? But within a few days he knew.

OPEN

Sometimes only afterward do we realize the significance of a particular event. Describe a situation like that that's happened to you.

STUDY

1. *Read John 19:25-42.* What concern seems to be a pressing concern on Jesus' mind when he looks down at the few faithful followers still with him at the foot of his cross (vv. 26-27)?

2. This moment—the last time we meet Jesus' mother in the Gospel story—is full of a pathos all of its own. Think back to that story, early on in the Gospel, when Mary pointed out to Jesus that the wine had run out (2:3-4). She didn't understand, then, that his time hadn't yet come. She doesn't understand now that this was where it was all leading.

    What must Jesus' mother have been thinking and feeling as she watched him suffering and dying before her eyes?

3. In 19:28 Jesus says he is thirsty. Jesus has spoken of water many times previously in the Gospel. There is the "sign" of chapter 2, which we just mentioned. There is the long discussion about "living water" with the woman of Samaria, in chapter 4. Jesus offered her that "living water" and it was clear that he had it in abundant supply. Then, in chapter 6, he spoke of those who believed in him not

only never being hungry, but also never being thirsty. He amplified this in chapter 7, speaking exuberantly of the "living water" that was available for anyone who came to him. They could satisfy their thirst forever by believing in him. Indeed they would have "rivers of living water" springing up from within themselves.

In light of all of this, what is the significance of Jesus' statement in verse 28?

4. The word translated "It is finished" or "It's all done!" (v. 30) is actually a single word in the original language. It's a word that people would write on a bill after it had been paid. The bill is dealt with. The price has been paid. Yes, says John: and Jesus' work is now complete, in that sense and in every other. It is upon this finished, completed work that his people from that day to this can stake their lives.

What does it mean for us to stake our lives on the completed work of Jesus?

5. Why do the Judeans ask Pilate to take down the bodies of those who were being crucified (v. 31)?

6. Crucifixion was a form of prolonged torture that could take days. The only way suspended victims could breath was to push up on their legs to get some air. To shorten the process, the soldiers would break their legs. Suffocation followed quickly. When the soldiers

came to Jesus, he was already dead. The soldiers were puzzled. That was quick! Was he, perhaps, just faking? No Roman soldier would let a condemned criminal escape death. His own life would be forfeit if he did. So, just to be sure, he stuck his spear hard up into Jesus' ribs; either it would kill him, or it would prove he was already dead.

What happens when the soldier thrusts the spear into Jesus' side (v. 34)?

7. Why does John emphasize in verse 35 that he was an eyewitness to these particular events?

8. At the moment when the lambs are being killed in the temple (John is careful to tell us that it was Passover that day), Jesus himself dies as the true Messiah, the true Passover lamb, who takes away the sin of the world.

   What do the Passover regulations in Exodus 12:46 and Numbers 9:12 require and how is this related to what happens here in verse 33?

9. Read Zechariah 12:10-11, which is quoted in verse 37. How is the response in Zechariah also an appropriate response to this real death that brings real deliverance from sin?

10. What does Joseph of Arimathea—who has only secretly been following Jesus until now—request of Pilate in verse 38?

11. Joseph and Nicodemus brought a hundred pounds of spices (in our weight system, about eighty pounds): a hundred times the amount that Mary had poured over Jesus in Bethany (12:3), and that had caused people to grumble at the extravagance. It was the kind of quantity (and quality, for that matter) that you might use for a king.

Why would Joseph and Nicodemus want to give Jesus such a burial?

12. John, we may be sure, intends us to remember the last time we stood before a tomb. Jesus wept outside Lazarus' tomb (11:35), but when they rolled the stone away there was no smell of decomposition (11:41). Wait, John says to us. Watch with me through this sabbath, this quiet, sad rest. Wait for this, the final day, the seventh day, to pass. God rested on the seventh day. So must Jesus. But this whole book has been about new creation. Wait for the eighth day.

How does the silence, stillness and sadness of holy Saturday teach us to wait patiently on the Lord?

PRAY

Sit in stillness and silence before the Lord for a while, remembering the quiet sadness that followed the death of Jesus the Messiah. Pray that with Joseph and Nicodemus, you also may emerge from the shadows of fear into the full light of day, offering all that you have to worship and adore the true King for all the world to see. Give him thanks for his patience with you, and ask that he in turn will grant you the patience to wait through the sadness in eager expectation of what he will do next.

NOTE ON JOHN 19:34

Thrusting the spear into Jesus' side would either kill him (as the soldiers watched the victim jerk and expire from the stab) or prove he was already dead. It proved the latter. After death, the body fluids separate. The medical details have been interpreted in different ways, and we don't know whether the spear might not have pierced Jesus' heart. The point seems to be, though, that whereas a living body would have produced blood, a dead body, from somewhere in the chest or stomach, would produce a mixture of clotting blood and a watery substance. Jesus really was dead. Afterward some claimed Jesus never actually died, that he just fainted, that they took him down from the cross too soon. The writer of the Gospel says otherwise. He saw a death, and insists on the truth of his evidence.

THE RISEN JESUS

John 20

Before the first time I went to stay with a family in Germany, I learned that when people say "you" in German, there are two forms, like the old English "ye" (for more than one person) and "thou" (for just one). In Germany it is polite to call everyone you meet by the plural word, "Sie." You only use the singular word, "Du," when talking to little children.

Until, that is, they tell you otherwise. The family I stayed with made me extremely welcome, looked after me and put up with my stumbling attempts to speak their language. I always called them "Sie." After several days my host, at supper, made a quiet announcement. I had been with them for some while now, and we had got to know one another. It was now appropriate that I should call them "Du." This was a new stage of friendship and intimacy. The nearest we come to it in English is, I suppose, when someone you have been calling "Dr. Smith" or "Mr. Jones" insists that instead you should call him or her by their first name.

This passage gives us a moment like that. It's a moment when it becomes clear that something extraordinary has taken place, not only to Jesus—though that's extraordinary enough—but to the way the world is, the way God is, the way God and the disciples now are. Up to this point Jesus has spoken about God as "the Father" and his followers as "disciples," "servants" and friends. Now verse 17: "Go to *my brothers* and say to them, 'I'm going up to my father *and your father*—to my God *and your God*.'"

OPEN

How do you know when you have moved from a formal relationship to more of a friendship? What indications are there of the shift? Up to this point Jesus has spoken about God as "The Father" and his followers as "disciples," "servants" and friends. Now all that changes in this chapter as he says to Mary in verse 17: "Go to *my brothers* and say to them, 'I'm going up to my father *and your father*—to my God *and your God*.'"

STUDY

1. *Read John 20:1-18.* What was Mary Magdalene's immediate reaction to seeing the stone rolled away from Jesus' tomb (vv. 1-2)?

2. The younger man, the beloved disciple, goes into the tomb after Peter. And the idea they had had to that point about what must have happened—someone taking the body away but unwrapping it first—suddenly looks stupid and irrelevant. Something quite new surges up in the young disciple.

   How does the faith expressed by the beloved disciple at this moment (v. 8) differ from the kind of faith the disciples had already shown in Jesus as the Messiah?

3. John tells us pointedly in verse 1 that this is the first day of the week, once again echoing the creation account of Genesis 1. How does Jesus' resurrection signal the beginning of God's new creation?

4. What does Mary say in an attempt to put words to her grief when the angels ask her why she's crying (v. 13)?

5. The angels ask Mary, "Why are you crying?" There are many today in grief and sadness. What answers would this question receive today if it were asked of you, your friends and family, and people all around the world?

6. How is Jesus' intimate presence an answer in those situations as it is in Mary's?

7. In light of John's echoes of Genesis 1 and his suggestion that this scene is the beginning of the new creation, how is it actually appropriate that Mary at first mistakes Jesus as the gardener (v. 15)?

8. If someone in the first century had wanted to invent a convincing story about people seeing Jesus, they wouldn't have dreamed about giving the star part to a woman. Let alone Mary Magdalene.

What does Mary's role in this story say about how God views the value of men and women in his new creation?

9. *Read John 20:19-31.* What does Jesus mean when he tells the disciples that he is sending them out just as the Father sent him (v. 21)?

10. The theme of new creation goes deeper still into this passage. The words for "wind," "breath" and "spirit" are the same (this is true in both Hebrew and Greek). This takes us back to the moment of creation itself. In Genesis 2:7 God breathed into human nostrils his own breath, the breath of life, and humankind came alive, alive with God's new life. Now, in the new creation, the restoring life of God is breathed out through Jesus (v. 22), making new people of the disciples, and, through them, offering this new life to the world.

In what practical ways can we carry out Jesus' commission to "forgive" and "retain" sins (v. 22)—that is, to extend Jesus' forgiveness to others, while yet warning the world that sin is a serious, deadly disease?

11. Thomas, the dour, dogged disciple who suggested they might as well go with Jesus, if only to die with him (11:16), who complained that Jesus hadn't made things anything like clear enough (14:5), just happened to be the one who was somewhere else on Easter day. He sees the others excited, elated, unable to contain their joy. He's not going to be taken in. He'll require hard, physical evidence to believe (v. 25).

What is the significance of Thomas's exclamation in verse 28?

12. The resurrection is not only *new* creation. It is new *creation*. To grasp this is vital to the health of the Christian faith. Any sense that Jesus starts a movement which is somehow opposed to, or can leave behind, the world which God made in the first place is excluded by this Gospel from start to finish.

How might we more intentionally live in a way that honors the created world as something that God deemed worthy of rescuing and renewing?

PRAY

As we stand there and listen, overhearing Mary's conversation with the angels in the garden, let the pain of the people you're with speak itself to Jesus, whether or not they know who he is. Then listen for the name. Let Jesus call your own name, and the name of whoever you've brought with you, whoever needs his love and healing today. Then rejoice and give thanks to God for raising Jesus from the dead and bringing to birth the new creation.

NOTE ON JOHN 20:17

The most puzzling feature of the passage is Jesus' warning to Mary in verse 17, "Don't cling to me," or as some translations say, "Don't touch me." Some have thought that his resurrection body was so new, so different, that he didn't want Mary trying to touch him and getting the wrong idea, thinking he was a ghost. That seems hardly likely in view of the other accounts, and the subsequent invitation to Thomas to touch and see.

I think it is more likely that it was a warning to Mary that the new relationship with him was not going to be like the old one. He wouldn't be going around sharing regular meals, discussing, talking, praying. They would see him now and then, but soon it would be time for him to "go to the father." Jesus was saying, "Don't try to keep me, to possess me." Mary is not upset by this. She doesn't feel it as a rebuff. She has business at hand. Jesus has given her an urgent task, and she gets on with it.

26

BREAKFAST BY THE SHORE

John 21

He had offered to help clear up after the dinner party. Indeed he was eager to do so. We gave him a towel and he worked away with us, wiping pans and jugs. But he was still excited after the events of the day, and his mind wasn't really on the job. Once or twice we suggested he might like to sit down, to read or relax. But he wanted to go on.

Then it happened. He picked up the new crystal water jug that we'd been given a few weeks before. He began to wipe it, but as he did so he turned round to say something to the others. He didn't notice one of them turning toward him at the same moment . . . until it was too late.

He was crestfallen. We were devastated but tried not to show it. He swept up the broken glass off the floor. He promised to buy us another jug. He left, a little later, in a flood of apologies.

We struggled to think through what forgiveness would mean in a case like that. We were angry, of course, but we knew it had happened because he was just too eager for his own good. We thought about it a lot. Then, a couple weeks later, we invited him to a meal again. And this time, after the meal, we invited him to help us clear up. Again we gave him a towel. He looked at us with a stare of unbelief. We smiled. He helped. It was fine.

This scene between Jesus and Peter is one of the most spectacular interchanges in the whole Bible, perhaps in all literature. Most remarkable is that, by way of forgiveness, Jesus gives Peter a job to do.

OPEN

What is the most meaningful act of forgiveness you've ever been shown by a person you've wronged?

STUDY

1. *Read John 21:1-25.* What did Jesus find the disciples unsuccessfully attempting to do on the morning described here (vv. 3-4)?

2. What point might John be making about the work we set out to do in the world and Jesus' involvement in that work (vv. 4-6)?

3. In your mind's eye stand with the disciples in the boat. What projects have you been laboring over and getting nowhere?

4. Jesus is already cooking fish and bread on his charcoal fire (v. 9). He doesn't need their catch. So why does Jesus tell the disciples to bring some of their fish over as well (v. 10)?

5. John specifically mentions a "charcoal fire" in verse 9. Look at the last time we encountered a charcoal fire in John's Gospel (see 18:18). Why is this a significant detail here?

6. Why does Jesus ask Peter the same question three times (vv. 15-17)?

7. Jesus goes to where the pain is, as he so often does. He takes Simon Peter away from the others. They are probably walking slowly along the shore. And he asks the question that goes to the heart of it all, "Do you love me?" The question is asked and answered; and even more, that answer earns not a pat on the back, not a "There, that's all right then," but a command. A fresh challenge. A new commission.

    How does the new commission that Jesus gives Peter offer a concrete way of demonstrating he's been forgiven and express hope for him?

8. How has Jesus specifically addressed the areas of your life that have needed forgiveness and healing?

9. Jesus tells Peter that he is going to have to follow him, not only in being a shepherd to the flock, but in glorifying God through dying as a martyr (vv. 18-19). It is the most natural thing in the world that he should ask Jesus whether John will share in this fate too.

Why does Jesus deny Peter the information he's looking for?

10. What misunderstanding does John seek to clear up by including this conversation about his own fate here (v. 23)?

11. Once the Word has become flesh, all the books in the world can't do justice to it. Nothing less than flesh can now do justice to the meaning of the Word: your flesh, my flesh. Books can reach a small way out into the world. Our lives, in the power of the Spirit, can reach a lot further.

   In what ways can your life become a living expression of the love of God for the world?

PRAY

Take a moment to imagine the relief and the new sense of purpose Peter must have felt after his time with Jesus on the shore. Now give thanks to God for extending to you that same kind of forgiveness and giving you a commission to serve him as well. Pray that you might know what it means to follow Christ wholeheartedly—even when it leads to pain and suffering—and that your life might be a faithful living expression of his love for all to see.

GUIDELINES FOR LEADERS

My grace is sufficient for you.
(2 Corinthians 12:9)

If leading a small group is something new for you, don't worry. These sessions are designed to flow naturally and be led easily. You may even find that the studies seem to lead themselves!

This study guide is flexible. You can use it with a variety of groups—students, professionals, coworkers, friends, neighborhood or church groups. Each study takes forty-five to sixty minutes in a group setting.

You don't need to be an expert on the Bible or a trained teacher to lead a small group. These guides are designed to facilitate a group's discussion, not a leader's presentation. Guiding group members to discover together what the Bible has to say and to listen together for God's guidance will help them remember much more than a lecture would.

There are some important facts to know about group dynamics and encouraging discussion. The suggestions listed below should equip you to effectively and enjoyably fulfill your role as leader.

PREPARING FOR THE STUDY

1. Ask God to help you understand and apply the passage in your own life. Unless this happens, you will not be prepared to lead others. Pray too for the various members of the group. Ask God to open

your hearts to the message of his Word and motivate you to action.

2. Read the introduction to the entire guide to get an overview of the topics that will be explored.

3. As you begin each study, read and reread the assigned Bible passage to familiarize yourself with it. This study guide is based on the For Everyone series on the New Testament (published by SPCK and Westminster John Knox). It will help you and the group if you have on hand a copy of the companion volume from the For Everyone series both for the translation of the passage found there and for further insight into the passage.

4. Carefully work through each question in the study. Spend time in meditation and reflection as you consider how to respond.

5. Write your thoughts and responses in a notebook or personal journal. This will help you to express your understanding of the passage clearly.

6. It may help to have a Bible dictionary handy. Use it to look up any unfamiliar words, names or places. The glossary at the end of each New Testament for Everyone commentary may likewise be helpful for keeping discussion moving.

7. Reflect seriously on how you need to apply the Scripture to your life. Remember that the group members will follow your lead in responding to the studies. They will not go any deeper than you do.

LEADING THE STUDY

1. At the beginning of your first time together, explain that these studies are meant to be discussions, not lectures. Encourage the members of the group to participate. However, do not put pressure on those who may be hesitant to speak—especially during the first few sessions.

2. Be sure that everyone in your group has a study guide. Encourage the group to prepare beforehand for each discussion by reading the introduction to the guide and by working through the questions in each study.

3. Begin each study on time. Open with prayer, asking God to help the group to understand and apply the passage.

4. Have a group member read aloud the introduction at the beginning of the discussion.

5. Discuss the "Open" question before the Bible passage is read. The "Open" question introduces the theme of the study and helps group members to begin to open up, and can reveal where our thoughts and feelings need to be transformed by Scripture. Reading the passage first will tend to color the honest reactions people would otherwise give—because they are, of course, supposed to think the way the Bible does. Encourage as many members as possible to respond to the "Open" question, and be ready to get the discussion going with your own response.

6. Have a group member read aloud the passage to be studied as indicated in the guide.

7. The study questions are designed to be read aloud just as they are written. You may, however, prefer to express them in your own words.

    There may be times when it is appropriate to deviate from the study guide. For example, a question may have already been answered. If so, move on to the next question. Or someone may raise an important question not covered in the guide. Take time to discuss it, but try to keep the group from going off on tangents.

8. Avoid answering your own questions. An eager group quickly becomes passive and silent if members think the leader will do most of the talking. If necessary repeat or rephrase the question until it is clearly understood, or refer to the commentary woven into the guide to clarify the context or meaning.

9. Don't be afraid of silence in response to the discussion questions. People may need time to think about the question before formulating their answers.

10. Don't be content with just one answer. Ask, "What do the rest of you think?" or "Anything else?" until several people have given answers to the question.

11. Try to be affirming whenever possible. Affirm participation. Never reject an answer; if it is clearly off-base, ask, "Which verse led you to that conclusion?" or again, "What do the rest of you think?"

12. Don't expect every answer to be addressed to you, even though this will probably happen at first. As group members become more at ease, they will begin to truly interact with each other. This is one sign of healthy discussion.

13. Don't be afraid of controversy. It can be very stimulating. If you don't resolve an issue completely, don't be frustrated. Explain that the group will move on and God may enlighten all of you in later sessions.

14. Periodically summarize what the group has said about the passage. This helps to draw together the various ideas mentioned and gives continuity to the study. But don't preach.

15. Conclude your time together with the prayer suggestion at the end of the study, adapting it to your group's particular needs as appropriate. Ask for God's help in following through on the applications you've identified.

16. End on time.